nas

Sociology for Nurses

D0773907

nas

Anatomy and Physiology for Nurses
Geriatric Nursing
Mathematics in Nursing
Medical Investigations
Medical Nursing
Microbiology for Nurses
Multiple Choice Questions, Book 1
Multiple Choice Questions, Book 2
Multiple Choice Questions, Book 3
Obstetric and Gynaecological Nursing
Paediatric Nursing
Personal and Community Health
Pharmacology for Nurses
Practical Nursing
Practical Procedures for Nurses
Psychiatric Nursing
Psychology for Nurses
Sociology for Nurses
Surgical Nursing
Theatre Technique

nas

Sociology for Nurses

Christine M. Chapman
OBE, BSc(Soc.), MPhil, SRN, SCM, RNT, FRCN
Professor of Nursing Education and Director of Nursing Studies,
University of Wales College of Medicine,
Cardiff, Wales

Third Edition

Baillière Tindall London Philadelphia Toronto
Mexico City **Sydney** **Tokyo** **Hong Kong**

Baillière Tindall: 33 The Avenue
                      Eastbourne, East Sussex BN21 3UN, England

                      West Washington Square
                      Philadelphia, PA 19105, USA

                      1 Goldthorne Avenue
                      Toronto, Ontario M8Z 5T9, Canada

                      Apartado 26370 — Cedro 512
                      Mexico 4, D.F., Mexico

                      ABP Australia Ltd, 44 Waterloo Road
                      North Ryde, NSW 2064, Australia

                      Ichibancho Central Building, 22-1 Ichibancho
                      Chiyoda-ku, Tokyo 102, Japan

                      10/FL, Inter-Continental Plaza, 94 Granville Road
                      Tsim Sha Tsui East, Kowloon, Hong Kong

First published 1977
Second edition 1982

Typeset by Multiplex Techniques Ltd
Printed in Great Britain by William Clowes (Beccles) Ltd

British Library Cataloguing in Publication Data
Chapman, Christine M.
    Sociology for nurses.—3rd ed.—(Nurses'
    aids series)
    1. Sociology   2. Nursing—Social aspects
    I. Title   II. Series
    301′.024613   HM51

    ISBN 0-7020-1188-6

Contents

	Preface	vii
	Preface to Third Edition	ix
1	Sociological Perspective	1
2	Methods of Study	7
3	The World of the Patient	16
4	The Role of the Patient and the Nurse	34
5	The Hospital as an Organization	49
6	Work and Life-styles	72
7	Gender in Society and Health Care	102
8	Nursing as an Occupation	113
9	Perceiving the Situation	134
10	Life Events and Illness	159
11	Power and Politics	167
12	Social Change	178
	Appendix	201
	Glossary	203
	Index	211

Preface

As John Donne has so succinctly put it 'no man is an island' and therefore no consideration of an individual, whether sick or well, is of value unless he is seen in his social setting. This setting and the inevitable pressures or constraints that it produces are the subject matter of sociology. Therefore the aim of this book on sociology for nurses is to provide an introduction to some basic sociological concepts and to show how they affect life in Britain today, and in particular the activity of nursing.

In a book of this nature it is not possible to discuss all sociological theories, and therefore the selection of those used is obviously the responsibility of the author. The further reading suggested at the end of each chapter will enable other viewpoints to be considered. Where possible, examples of the concepts in action are taken from the field of health care, and demographic material relates entirely to Britain.

This is not a book for the purist, as it includes material which may be considered sociological theory, social administration, and in some cases medical and/or nursing sociology, in order that nurses may better understand the lives of their patients and hence be able to provide more effective care.

In order to assist understanding of technical terms, many of which are used in ordinary conversation, the first time a word is used it is printed in italics and an explanation of such terms is found in the glossary.

Some of the material is based on lectures given to students of the Bachelor of Nursing Degree at Cardiff. For their involuntary help I thank them. However the book is not meant only to meet the needs of undergraduate nurses but to be of use to both the student nurse and the RGN.

I gratefully acknowledge permission to reproduce material as follows: Figs 5 and 6, and Tables 7, 11, 12, 13 and 14 to HMSO; Table 8 to McIntosh and Woodley; Table 9 to J. Goldthorpe and D. Lockwood; Table 10 to OPCS; Figs 13 and 14 to John Wiley & Sons taken from *Toward a Theory of Nursing* by I.M. King. HMSO material is reproduced with the permission of the Controller of Her Majesty's Stationery Office.

My thanks are also due to many other people with whom I have discussed specific portions and in particular I should like to thank Mrs C. Pritchard, my secretary, who has achieved the near impossible by deciphering my handwriting and typing the results.

Christine M. Chapman
September 1977

Preface to Third Edition

The favourable response to the first and second editions of this introductory textbook has resulted in this third edition. In the eight years that have elapsed since the first edition, nursing has been characterized by an increasing awareness of the individuality of the patient. This has been demonstrated by the increasing use of the Nursing Process as a tool to ensure individualized patient care. As in the first edition, the aim of this book is to alert nurses to the effect that being a member of society has on individuals and how, as collections of individuals, they form society. What is true for the patient is equally true for the nurse, and it is hoped that understanding of each other will increase meaningful interaction and also help in raising and maintaining the quality of nursing care.

Obviously it is not possible to update concepts and theory, so much of the book remains the same. Examples have, where appropriate, been updated and so have some of the tables. Two new chapters have been added. One on 'Gender in Society and Health Care' and the other on 'Power and Politics'.

Readers should note the comments in the preface to the first edition, that this is very much an introduction to sociology for nurses; further reading is essential for complete understanding and the suggested reading at the end of each chapter has been increased and updated. Acknowledgement is due to my secretary, Mrs Eileen Webb, who has assisted with the typing.

Christine M. Chapman
October 1985

1 Sociological Perspective

Everyone has at some point in their life found themselves in a gathering of people and experienced the feeling of 'not belonging'. Why? — They are physically the same as the others; their clothes are appropriate for the situation; they are not even being ignored — on the contrary people talk to them and yet still there is the feeling of being uncomfortable in the group. In another context most people, even those with no Christian allegiance, find themselves talking in whispers in an empty church. Throughout the world children play at 'being' doctors and nurses, form gangs and scream after pop idols. In the West boy meets girl, admires and dates her, falls in love and marries. In the East the bride is led to marry a man chosen by her parents whom she has never seen. Why this sense of pressure from people or institutions, why is so much behaviour predictable and yet what causes one country to have one pattern of behaviour and another a completely different one? These are some of the questions that sociology tries to answer.

The word 'sociology' was coined by Auguste Comte (1838) and is a barbaric combination of Latin and Greek, meaning a study of society on a generalized or abstract level. The object of the study is man (human beings) existing and acting in interdependence; what happens when man meets man, when human beings form groups, cooperate, fight, persuade or imitate others, develop or destroy communities and cultures. This concern can be with whole societies or institutions, that is a *macroscopic view*, or with small groupings of two or three people which is a *microscopic view*. There are many disciplines which study man and it is important to consider sociology and its relationship with these subjects.

Biological sciences

Anatomy and physiology and associated disciplines study the structure and functioning of man. Obviously a man's biological make-up will affect his behaviour in some areas of life. It is unlikely that a 100-kg man will become a ballet dancer, he is more likely to be found in the pack of a rugby team. However, whether he becomes a Voodoo man or a Fellow of the Royal College of Surgeons is likely to depend more upon his country of birth than on his physique. Even some of the things that we assume are 'natural' are in fact learned. Many would assert that female behaviour is entirely the result of the possession of a specific female form and the action of female hormones, yet over the world females behave differently.. Compare the women warriors of the Amazon with those in colourful saris in India. Quite apart from Women's Liberation movements, Western society in the past sixty years has shown (largely as a result of two world wars) that women are capable of successfully filling the same jobs as men, apart from those requiring excessive physical strength.

Psychology

There is a close relationship between sociology and psychology in that the basic unit of society is the individual and psychology is concerned with the behaviour and mental processes of individuals. Both are therefore concerned with individuals but at a different level of analysis: the psychologist mainly with man as an individual, the sociologist with the individual as part of a social system. However, the two disciplines become linked in social psychology and in some specific theories in sociology.

Social anthropology

At one time social anthropology was mainly concerned with the study of pre-literate societies. However, as the number of these societies shrinks, culture in all types of societies is being studied and therefore both the area of investigation and the techniques used tend to overlap with studies in comparative sociology.

History

History is a study of human past as a sequence of concrete and unique events, situations and processes, how and why. Each event is unique and history shows the variables while sociology is concerned with showing the constant and recurring events and their links with other phenomena existing at the same time. Again lines of demarcation are blurred, but sociology concentrates mainly on the present rather than on the past.

Social philosophy

Social philosophy is primarily an attempt to understand the world in its totality and to develop ultimate principles, for example, What is good? Society is explained, not in terms of observed facts as in sociology but in terms of the explanations given, supreme values and ultimate ends. Again the boundaries between sociology and philosophy are often crossed and the same methods may be used.

Geography

When geography is concerned with the social aspects of environment and ways of life it is closely akin to sociology.

Economics

Economics tends to study human actions defined by their goals and is aimed at solution of material problems. Again there are areas of overlap in that economic problems may pattern society's activity.

Political science

Political science investigates the acquisition and exertion of *power*, not only by governments but also by subgroups and as such is one aspect of *social structure* and the way society exerts control over its members.

To summarize, the sociologist Piterim Sorokin states: 'That if within a class of phenomena there are '*n*' subclasses, then there must be $n + 1$ disciplines to study them; n to study each of the subclasses and one more to study what is common to all and their correlation; this is the position of sociology which investigates all types of human activity.'

Terminology

One of the problems of the student coming fresh to the study of sociology is that many words used in ordinary speech become endowed with special meaning in the mouth of the sociologist, that is they become technical terms. Frequently these words describe *concepts* which are the building bricks of *theory*. A concept can be described as a mental image formed by generalizing impressions received from the senses. It is abstract and symbolic but, once accepted, conveys a wealth of feeling and understanding and becomes a unit of thought. It is true that experience may produce a slightly different mental picture for each individual, but nevertheless it is a useful and universal method of communication. Terms such as family, home, love, nurse, by producing a mental image remove the need to embark on a long description of the topic under discussion.

The term 'theory' is applied to interrelationships of ideas or concepts and theories are used as intellectual tools which are formulated to show connections between observable factors which might otherwise be thought to exist in isolation. One important aspect of theory is that it is capable of proof by *empirical* means. Merton says 'Concepts, then, constitute the definitions of what is to be observed; they are the variables between which empirical relationships are to be sought. When propositions are logically interrelated, a theory has been instituted.'

Concepts therefore form a basic vocabulary with which people can communicate. This is not a new idea for nurses who frequently learn abstract generalizations; for example the word *shock* has a technical meaning for a nurse who may understand its meaning and implication without ever having seen a patient experiencing it. Naturally the image is clearer once the condition has been seen. It is also an example of a word having a lay as well as a technical meaning, implying astonishment for the man in the street, a physiological state to a nurse, and a physical state to an electrician. If then a basic vocabulary of concepts is used to enable nurses to communicate with each other easily and specifically, it is not surprising that the same is true of other disciplines including sociology.

Initially it may be a little difficult to appreciate the nuances that make the use of these words more precise than when employed in ordinary conversation. Most of these terms relate to what Emile Durkheim, one of the founding fathers of sociology, calls *social facts*. He defines social facts as ways of acting, thinking and feeling which are general in a society and which exert pressure on individuals in the society to conform. This implies that individual behaviour is to some extent the result of outside pressure and not completely controlled by the individual's consciousness. Durkheim in fact says that: 'The determining cause of a social fact should be sought among the social facts preceding it and not among the state of the individual consciousness.'

Although sociologists today do not deny the pressures exerted on individuals by society they also take account of the individual's perception of society and the way he *defines the situation*. Most people will have had the experience of being in a situation with colleagues and being amazed to find that while one person perceives it as a permissive environment, another finds it threatening. Each individual then acts according to the way he interprets the facts, one with ease and freedom, the other guardedly and with suspicion.

Finally there is the concept of *dynamism* in any situation; because society is made up of interacting individuals it can never be exactly the same over time. Just as an actor in a play may put over different aspects of a character so individuals may one day be optimistic, another gloomy, and this will affect those with whom they come in contact. A situation which one day may be one of cheerful cooperation may on another day (apparently identical) involve conflict and acrimony — not a new idea to a nurse who finds the care of every patient different although they may have the same disease and receive identical treatment.

References and Further Reading

Berger, P.L. (1966) *Invitation to Sociology*. Harmondsworth: Pelican.

Coulson, M.A. & Riddel, C. (1970) *Approaching Sociology*. London: Routledge & Kegan Paul.

Cox, C. (1981) A sociological perspective. In Smith, J.P. (ed.) *Nursing Science and Nursing Practice*. London: Butterworths.

Nisbet, R.A. (1967) *The Sociological Tradition*. London: Heinemann.

Worsley, P. (1977) *Introduction to Sociology*. Harmondsworth: Penguin.

Worsley, P. (ed.) (1977) *Modern Sociology, Introductory Readings*. Part I. Harmondsworth: Penguin.

2 Methods of Study

Sociologists are often taunted by members of other disciplines with the accusation that their studies are not 'scientific'. If by this they mean that society cannot be 'experimented with' in the same way as metals or if they are highlighting the fact that it is impossible to replicate exactly any given situation and therefore 'prove' a theory again, this is indisputable. However, philosophers debate the level at which anything can be 'proved' and sociologists frequently use a 'scientific method' in formulating theory.

Development of theory usually starts with the observation of factors in society which either persist or change and this arouses curiosity and the question 'why?' After a period of thinking round this problem the investigator usually comes up with a suggested answer or tentative theory as a statement which is called a *hypothesis*. The next step is to test the hypothesis by examining the various concepts associated with it, amassing appropriate data followed by analysis of the results so that confirmation or rejection of the original statement is possible. If the hypothesis is confirmed, then it needs to be retested in other situations, possibly other countries and cultures, until it is seen to be such a reliable statement that it can be used as a theory. Emile Durkheim was the first sociologist to use this method. He believed that society exerted a pressure on individuals in such a way that many of the activities that an individual felt were entirely under the control of his will were, in fact, determined by the society in which he lived. At this time he observed that the suicide rate in any given society tended to remain constant over time although it varied between societies, this despite the fact that suicide was and is generally considered to be a highly personal act. Linking his observations with the theory postulated by Freud that suicide is dependent on neurotic traits, Durkheim looked for a cultural *group* which was considered to have a high level of neurotic traits and decided to study the Jews. He formulated the hypothesis that Jews would have a higher suicide rate than other groups due to their neurotic personality. However, having studied the appropriate data he found that this was not so and that they had a comparatively low rate of suicide. He became curious about the factors existing amongst Jews that might account for the surprisingly low rate and he found that Jewish communities were such tightly knit groups that individuals felt secure and integrated in their communities. This he describes as a high level of *social integration*.

The next step in the investigation was to use this concept of social integration to test other groups to see if levels of integration could be ascertained and if so whether social integration could be used as an indicator of suicide susceptibility in societies. This Durkheim did and was able by his studies to demonstrate that individuals are profoundly affected by the sense with which they feel they 'belong' in a society. He was also able to show that part of this belonging was related to the level at which people felt they knew what society expected of them, that is, how well they understood society's *norms* or rules. (Norms are the recognized ways of behaving in a society, they may be backed by laws but usually are unwritten rules which people keep in order to be accepted.)

As a result of these findings Durkheim postulated three situations where the individual might commit suicide. One of these he called *altruistic* suicide which would occur when the individual felt that society would benefit from his death. An example might be the Japanese kamikaze pilot of the Second World War who felt that death would be a contribution to his country. Another example would be that of 'suttee', the Hindu widow, throwing herself on the funeral pyre of her husband rather than be a burden to her relatives in a society which had no place or provision for a woman on her own. A second situation he described was when people felt that they had nothing to contribute to society or society to them. This group he called *egoistic*. The third group he said was made up of people who felt lost in society in that they did not know what was required of them or what they could contribute, in other words they did not understand society's norms. Durkheim was able to demonstrate that this type of suicide tended to occur in societies that were undergoing rapid change, resulting in norms being discarded which, until replaced, led individuals to feel 'lost'. Although some people were able to tolerate this break in security others could not, nor could they adapt to the new situation. The resulting situation, called by Durkheim *anomie*, made such individuals feel life was not worth living. Although subsequent work has questioned some of Durkheim's findings, the method he used in his investigations remains much the same and is used by researchers today.

METHODS OF INVESTIGATION

The hypothesis is the formulation of the tentative theory, often in negative terms, for example, 'There is no difference between the level of anxiety demonstrated by men or women undergoing surgery for varicose veins.' Sometimes if there are a large number of points to be tested there may have to be several hypotheses, each dealt with separately although the findings may be put together in the final analysis.

Sampling

Having decided on the area of study as indicated by the hypothesis a decision has to be made as to whether all the appropriate people should be covered or only some of them. Obviously the number studied must be large enough to provide adequate statistical data, and if a sample is chosen it must be representative of the total relevant population. Samples can be completely *random*, so that each person in the total population has an equal chance of being picked until the final number is complete. An example of this method is picking names out of a hat, while researchers use a technique of random numbers. Quasi random, for example choosing every tenth person in a series, can be used, but once this decision has been made persons numbered 1–9, 11–19, and so on, are excluded even before the second person has been selected. A *convenience sample* may be used and an example could be the first fifty people to attend a specific clinic. A *stratified sample* implies the selection from different groups to ensure that they are all represented. An example would be taking ten persons from different age ranges such as 20–29 years, 30–39 years, or grading by other means such as *social class*.

Observation

Because societies are made up of living, functioning, interacting individuals, one way in which they may be studied is by observation. This can be done by the observer standing outside the group and recording all he sees and hears. However, there are problems. It is a common experience that if we are aware of being watched then we tend to behave differently, although it has been shown that if the observer is there for a sufficiently long period of time, then he blends into the background, people cease to be aware of him and behave less self-consciously. A more difficult problem is that of understanding what is seen and heard. Take, for example, a ward sister talking to a patient. This may be idle chat about a knitting pattern, a piece of instruction, information giving or receiving, reassurance, or a mixture of them all. If the observer merely records 'talking to patient', then a great deal of meaningful material is lost. Equally, if a lay person observes a physiotherapist percussing a patient's back, he may well record 'slapping' but not know whether it is punitive, therapeutic or fun! These problems can be overcome to some extent if the observer is also a participant in the activity. This will enable an understanding of the context and therefore it is more likely that the meaning of the action will be correctly interpreted. However, by being part of the activity the participant may consciously or unconsciously alter it. This has been shown to be a very real problem when the interaction being observed is between two people, as in district nursing or health visiting (Kratz, 1974). An added problem is that it is difficult to be dispassionate when actually involved in the situation and the observer may be tempted to interfere in a situation, especially if it appears that people may suffer. For example it would be difficult to stand by and watch a patient fall out of bed!

The role of observer therefore can be anywhere on a *continuum*, as shown:

Observer   Observer/Patient   Participant/Observer   Participant

All of these methods are time-consuming for the investigator although they may yield a great deal of information, and indeed be the only possible approach when a completely new area is being studied, but often information can be collected in other ways. An interesting account of this method is found in a book by J. Roth called *Timetables* in which he describes being a participant observer in a tuberculosis hospital. He did this as a patient, as an attendant and as a sociological researcher.

Questionnaires

Most readers will at some time or other be asked to complete one of these. They can be a list of questions to be answered, either completely freely: 'How do you think the ward off-duty should be arranged?' or with a structured answer: 'Do you think the ward off-duty should be arranged to cover — (tick appropriate box)

> one week   ☐
> one month   ☐
> three months   ☐
> other (please state)'

There may be other variations to this type of question and the way in which it is presented. Since this type of questionnaire may be given to a large number of people there are obvious problems. The person receiving it must be literate and must understand the questions; he may have to be able to recall information; give an opinion on a subject about which he knows very little; or, if honest, incriminate himself. The way the question is asked may influence the answer or the question may be ambiguous or embarrassing. Unless the investigator hands out the questionnaire and waits while it is completed it may be pushed to one side and forgotten.

There are ways in which some of these problems can be overcome and one of them is to link a questionnaire with the next method, the interview.

Interview

The interview may seem self-explanatory but as with the questionnaire there are variations. Here the investigator meets his subject in a face-to-face situation and asks the questions. This may be a completely unstructured discussion of a topic with the interviewer either using a tape recorder or making notes afterwards or it may be structured round a questionnaire which is filled in by the interviewer.

As with all methods there are disadvantages, not least being the personality of the interviewer; the tone of voice and manner in which he asks the questions and the way in which he records the answers may produce *bias*.

Historical or other documents

Sometimes the information required by the investigator has already been collected; an example could be hospital activity figures such as bed occupancy. What is required then is that the relevant material is collected and put together prior to analysis. Unfortunately the way in which the material has been gathered or recorded may make its use difficult as details required by the investigator may have been irrelevant for the original user.

Demographic material
One special set of figures that are often used by sociologists are those relating to the social structure of the country such as birth rates, death rates, numbers of people employed in various occupations, numbers of houses owned or rented, how people spend their leisure time and so on. Some of these figures are collected annually, others only at the ten-yearly census.

These then are some of the tools of the investigator which may be combined or modified. The reader who requires detailed information on this subject should consult one of the texts listed at the end of this chapter.

USE OF FINDINGS

The investigator may give a descriptive account of the findings but not place any interpretation on the work. Alternatively the findings may be analysed using statistical techniques, either by hand or using a computer and the results presented in the form of tables, graphs, histograms or charts of various types, illustrating factors which occur together (*correlations*), percentages, averages, deviations and levels of *significance* (whether or not the findings could have occurred by chance). From these data it may be possible to show how the original hypothesis is supported or rejected.

MODELS

Another way in which society may be described is by the use of a *model*. In this case a situation, or apparatus, already understood is used to illustrate activities taking place in a society. A common example is the use of an organic model to describe society. Just as a living organism needs certain things in order to function, live, grow and reproduce, so society may be said to 'need' certain things if it is to continue to exist. This model uses terms like *homeostasis* to describe the way a society reacts to factors so that a state of equilibrium is maintained.

While models are useful their great danger is that they may be taken too literally so that, for example, if the organic model is used there is a danger of thinking that society *is* an organism. This activity is called *reification*.

COMPARATIVE METHOD

Experimentation is obviously difficult in society. Groups of human beings are not easily manipulated as experimental subjects. However it is possible in certain situations to find societies which are similar and then to observe the effect of the introduction of a variable in one using the other as a control. For example, two similar towns might be considered, and in one, laws controlling the selling of alcohol abolished, while retained in the other. Each might then be studied noting the amount of alcohol consumed, incidence of drunkenness, driving accidents, wife beating or other social phenomena. Obviously there are difficulties, the first being that of ensuring that the towns are really comparable. Next the indicators used to measure the effect of the changed laws may be the wrong ones, or they may be the result of some other unaccounted factor; in the above example the fact of the town's people being observed might account for changes in behaviour. Finally there is the ethical question — is it justifiable to subject one group of people to the dangers of alcoholism, increased road accidents or other dangerous activities?

Even though a hypothesis may have been refuted or supported it may need to be retested several times before evidence is sufficient to delineate a theory with confidence.

This account is of necessity very brief and the reader

interested in either carrying out an investigation or wishing to read research reports with more understanding should be aware that many topics have not been covered.

One of the problems of research in the sociological field is that of bias. Sociologists are human beings and when studying society cannot help but be influenced by their own experience and few can detach themselves from the social concerns of their times, be they poverty or war. Obviously as far as possible sociological research must be carried out in such a way as to be 'value-free', that is, free from bias. However, the use of research methods, and of insight into the material shown by the data, needs imagination and personal involvement. A sociologist has to try to be objective yet retain his humanity — he needs both head and heart.

References and Further Reading

Abdellah, G. & Levine, E. (1979) *Better Patient Care through Nursing Research*. London: Collier Macmillan.

Calnan, J. (1976) *One Way to Do Research. The A–Z for those who Must*. London: Heinemann.

Cicourel, A. (1964) *Method and Measurement in Sociology*. New York: Free Press.

Durkheim, E. (1952) *Suicide: A Study in Sociology*. London: Routledge & Kegan Paul.

Kratz, C.R. (1974) Problems in the care of the long-term sick in the community. Unpublished PhD thesis, University of Manchester.

Lancaster, A. et al (1975) *Guidelines to Research in Nursing*. London: King Edward Hospital Fund.

Mills, C. Wright (1970) *The Sociological Imagination*. Harmondsworth: Penguin.

Moser, C.A. & Kalton, G. (1971) *Survey Methods and Social Investigation*. London: Heinemann.

Popper, K.R. (1968) *The Logic of Scientific Discovery*. London: Hutchinson.

Roth, J. (1963) *Timetables: Structuring the Passage of Time in Hospital Treatment and Other Careers*. Indianapolis: Bobbs Merrill.

3 The World of the Patient

It is often difficult for a nurse to visualize the 'other world' of the patient: the world in the case of a man, where he is a husband, father, managing director, coalman or any other of the myriad positions that an individual may occupy. Once in bed, clothed in the ubiquitous chain store pyjamas or nightdress, the man or woman takes on the camouflage of 'patient', possibly subdivided into 'medical' or 'surgical' or with the disease label as a ticket of identification. Nevertheless it is the individual's life in the 'real' world that has made him what he now is — a patient. A 'good' patient or a 'difficult' patient will eventually return as father, managing director, or in the case of a female, mother, sweetheart, secretary, head mistress and so on.

THE FAMILY

These positions (or *roles*) that an individual occupies in life are first situated within the family and later extend into the world of school, work and social contacts. Despite the fact that we all have a family of origin, that is, the one into which we were born, families are not standard in either size or function and the variations will affect the roles played by the individual.

Some years ago a small boy, the son of a research worker living and working in the East End of London, was asked by his school teacher to draw his family. He did this, portraying mother, father and brother, but on returning home to his parents commented: 'Isn't it funny, the others were putting in their nannas and aunties and uncles and all sorts of people like that.' This story illustrates vividly the variation that exists within the United Kingdom over the definition of 'the family' and if the discussion is extended worldwide then the variations may be even more marked.

When sociologists wish to compare social phenomena which have wide variations they frequently use a device called the *ideal-type*, a tool first developed by Max Weber. An ideal-type is not, as might be supposed, the best, or even the average example, but is an abstract construct. In other words, if the characteristics of a certain activity or social institution are taken to their logical extreme, there is the 'ideal-type'. Max Weber emphasized that 'this mental construct cannot be found empirically anywhere in reality'. However it is theoretically possible that the traits may be found together.

When studying the family there are two-ideal-types to be considered. First there is the family that the little boy drew, a mother, father and their children living under one roof — this is the *nuclear family*. Secondly, there is the family consisting of a father and mother, their children (married and single) plus the families of their children (usually only the sons' families as when the daughters marry they go to join their husband's family). This type of family, which will therefore have grandparents, parents, siblings, aunts, uncles and cousins living under one roof, is called an *extended family*. Obviously the way these families live, work and cooperate will be different as will the functions that they perform. Many people feel that the extended family is the original family structure and that the nuclear family has developed in response to the needs of industrialization and modernization in society. However, this view is open to question, especially when normal length of life in pre-industrial societies is considered: in many cases people did not live long enough for three generations to live together.

The commencement of the family is the occasion of the marriage of two adults which alters their status in society, no longer single but married and therefore regarded differently and with new rights and duties — the *status passage*, from single to married, the nature of which may vary but its effect is the same in that it marks outwardly the change that has occurred. The occurrence of marriage may be as the result of economic bargaining as in societies where there is a 'bride price' or dowry or as the result of physical and/or emotional attraction and romantic love. In the first case it is usually arranged between parents, in the second, by the individuals themselves. Age of marriage may also vary and is often related to the inheritance of land as in peasant societies where the age of marriage is high, marriage being postponed until it can be 'afforded' in terms of land. (This also has the result of depressing the birth rate.) In other countries the age of marriage may be low, even occurring in childhood, as in India, although the participants will not consummate the ceremony until puberty. Indeed not to be married by fifteen years may be a public scandal, or the opposite may be true.

Apart from the economic, political or romantic aims of marriage, it provides for an approved sexual relationship coupled with the expectation of reproduction and normally involves common residence. Sexual relationships always have some sort of moral value attached to them. In some societies a girl will not be married until she is pregnant, in others virginity at marriage is regarded as desirable. Codes exist in societies defining legitimate sexual relations so that although 'incest' is a taboo that is found in most, nearness of the forbidden relationship varies. For example it is possible to marry a second cousin in the United Kingdom but not in some tribes. In the same way the number of wives permitted may vary. This is now an important point in Britain where having more than one wife is against the law yet some Moslem immigrants expect to be able to have up to four.

Birth rates tend to be most profoundly affected by the *neonatal* death rate. The more babies that are likely to die the greater the number that a family will try to have to ensure succession by a son, or sufficient sons to work the land in the case of agrarian communities. From the moment the baby is born his life is socially ordered and affected by the type of food he receives, methods of welcome into the society, hygiene, toys allowed and so on. Much of this is called *socialization* and is the way in which the new baby is helped to fit into the type of society into which he has been born.

Survival of the family as a unit is also socially controlled. In some societies divorce is merely a matter of mutual consent, in others attendance at a law court is necessary. The dowry may have to be returned in some cases, in others there may be complicated financial settlements such as alimony. Finally in societies which place a high value on marriage as a religious institution, divorce may be almost impossible.

Extended family

The extended family comprises three or four generations living together with social and economic cooperation, usually as the result of sons bringing their wives into the family on their marriage. Some form of organization and control has to develop and this is normally hierarchical, the grandfather (or in some cases the grandmother) being the family head. When the grandfather dies his eldest son then becomes the head of the family.

The extended family may be completely self-supporting and within its structure carry out all the functions necessary for survival, health and happiness. Children are socialized into their role and receive appropriate education by the family in order to fulfil their place in the family. Division of labour and responsibility for the economic requirements of the family will be carefully controlled by its head to ensure that each individual not only receives according to his needs but also makes an appropriate contribution to the common good. Due to the large number of adults available there will be division of function, not only in production (usually a male role) but also in care within the group. While some women will be responsible for cooking and housekeeping, others will be expected to care for small children or teach them specific skills, while others may take on the care of the sick or aged.

Social control of such a family is bound up with religious observance which often contains within it ideas of respect and reverence of ancestors. The head of the family may lead corporate acts of religious observance ranging from such activities as burning incense before household gods to the daily conduct of family prayers. Linked with this will be the exertion of discipline and control of *deviancy*. The views of the family are also united in that their political life usually reflects a desire to maintain the status quo. Political knowledge and practice is mainly the concern of the man and therefore included in the socialization programme of the boys of the family. The position of the aged in the family is secure. They receive deference due to their knowledge accumulated as a result of a longer life experience than the younger members. As physical or mental powers fade there will be gradual withdrawal from work or decision-making but there will not be a sudden severance from being a producer to being dependent and so anxiety over future care or status will not be prominent. Finally in such a family there is ample provision for leisure pursuits in that there are sufficient individuals in each generation for interests to be shared.

Nuclear family

In the nuclear family there are not more than two generations living together, the two adults, father and mother, and their unmarried children. Typically they do not live very near any of their relations but in a new area away from that of their origin (neolocal) and may often move at regular intervals as job opportunities change. Due to this geographic and social *mobility* there is less adherence to family traditions and obligations and a greater acceptance of change. Naturally this family carries out fewer functions than the extended family. The regulation of sexual relations in society, reproduction and primary socialization of children are still its concern but *secondary socialization*, education, religious and political functions are either shared or completely handed over to outside agencies. Health care and leisure provision are also only covered at an elementary level, the remainder being provided by the state. Social control other than at a very low level is also the concern of the state, hence the development of law enforcement agencies such as the police.

The question now arises as to why there should be this variation in family structure and function? Is it a change that inevitably occurs with modernization; in other words must an extended family be changed in order to 'fit' an industrial society? It is true that the ideal-type nuclear family is more frequently seen in industrial societies and the extended family in the underdeveloped countries but there is also evidence to show that this division is not as clear cut as might have been expected.

Although some extended families are mobile if hunting is their main means of support, most remain in the same geographical area and indeed often in the same dwelling for many centuries. Providing the source of food does not disappear, there is no pressure to move and equally, unless some outside force compels change, there is no impetus towards innovation. Industrial society, however, demands that the worker be able to go to where the work is. This geographic mobility can clearly be seen in Britain by the number of Scots, Welsh and Irish who left their homelands (often rural areas) to work in the manufacturing industries of Birmingham, Manchester, Liverpool and other big cities.

This severance of close ties with the families of origin of the husband and wife throws them more together. They tend to share duties, friends and interests to a greater degree than occurred in the extended family where the men would have congregated together while the women shared gossip in another room. This increase in involvement spreads also to the children so that there may be more time spent with them, both in play and by showing more concern over their education and friendships. At the same time more money is spent on the home and its contents to make it more comfortable. This will, however, frequently be small and there will be little room to care for any member of the family who is sick, handicapped or old. In a time of full employment both adult members of the family are likely to be employed outside the home and have little time to care for others apart from their dependent children and so industrial society has to provide the care that might have been given at home.

In Britain there is an increasing number of 'single-parent families' which do not fit into the continuum and which have special problems. Not only may there be economic difficulties – often the parent, whether male or female, needs to work yet may have to stay at home to care for the children – but there may be difficulties in socialization of the children as one role model, mother or father, is missing. These families need greater social provision, both in terms of money and in provision of crèches, nursery schools, etc. (Table 1).

Because employment is by an outside agency rules are formed which decide when an individual must cease work. These rules may be based on average physical and mental ability and also take into account the need to vacate jobs so that young people do not become blocked on the promotion ladder. This policy results in the *rites de passage* of retirement often accompanied by a presentation from firm and workmates (it is ironic that at the period of life when timekeeping is least important the presentation is often a clock). Apart from a few enlightened firms which allow a gradual rundown in working life, most people experience a sudden severance in *status*. One day one is a worker and economically independent and the next, retired and dependent on pension from state or firm or both. Accompanying this blow is the realization that there may be no possibility of care from family in case of illness or as age progresses, but that ultimately total care may have to be provided by the state in an old people's home. Many old people feel this situation deeply and resent being considered useless by society, especially when they are fit, mentally alert and capable of making a contribution.

Industrial societies therefore provide *institutions* to take

Table 1. One-parent families in Great Britain, by household composition*.

| | Marital status of lone mothers | | | | | | | | All lone mothers | | All lone fathers | | All one-parent families | |
| | Single | | Widowed | | Divorced | | Separated | | | | | | | |
	1973–75	1981–83	1973–75	1981–83	1973–75	1981–83	1973–75	1981–83	1973–75	1981–83	1973–75	1981–83	1973–75	1981–83
Household composition														
Living alone	36	56	88	88	74	84	78	80	72	77	70	82	72	78
Living with parents	49	32	7	3	15	5	13	8	18	11	11	8	17	11
Living with relatives	7	5	4	7	4	3	3	4	4	4	8	3	5	4
Living with non-relatives														
Male	7	4	2	3	7	7	5	5	5	5	1	2	5	5
Female	1	2	0	0	–	2	1	3	–	2	10	5	2	2
Sample size (=100%) (numbers)	182	298	256	196	350	578	302	287	1090	1359	183	165	1273	1524

*Based on relationship of lone parent to other family heads. Values are percentages of sample size.
Source: General Household Survey, combined data for 1973–1975 inclusive, and 1981–1983 inclusive.

over the functions of the family which in its nuclear form it can no longer fulfil; hence schools, banks, markets, police, law courts, organized religion, hospitals, social service and welfare provisions. Students of history will know, however, that many of these institutions existed prior to industrialization and so there is the 'chicken–egg' question of which came first.

Social history also shows that amongst the working class in Britain the nuclear family is not new but has been in existence more or less since records began. It is true that amongst the aristocracy or upper class the extended family flourished and may still survive today, but the peasant farmer was rarely able to support more than his immediate family. Therefore, as far as Britain is concerned, there is evidence to indicate that family structure and function are much more related to social class and culture than just to the occurrence of industrialization. One solution to this diversity of opinion may be due to the way in which the ideal-type family is defined. If to qualify as an extended family all the members must live under one roof, then it is true that there are few left in the United Kingdom at this time. However, if the concept of mutual support, cooperation and ties of affection are considered, then studies show that these remain. Some studies of working-class families show that although the children move out from the family home on marriage, they do not move far. In fact in Bethnal Green in East London, Young and Wilmott (1969) found that often the mother speaks to the rent collector asking that any vacant house in the area be allocated to the child (most frequently daughter) about to marry. If the family is known to be reliable over payments, the house owners often consider the child will probably be the same and therefore a good tenant. As a result married children often live in the same street or the next one to their parents. This geographic proximity allows the mutual help and support to be continued, particularly amongst the women. The mother will care for the daughter when her children are born, while the daughter will shop for her mother or do her washing. On Sundays the children and their families tend to 'go home' to see their parents and so contact is kept with siblings and their children grow up having regular contact with aunts, uncles and cousins. Traditional family activities, stories and legends are passed on to succeeding generations and there is a sense of 'belonging' to the extended family network. The person who acts as the hub of the network in the working class is the mother and on her death there tends to be a breakdown in family cohesion and a drifting apart. In middle-class families there is less likelihood of children being near their parents but the possession of the telephone and/or car may ensure that contact is maintained. Because of the distances involved support in kind may be less but there is evidence to show that this is replaced by financial help and support: grandparents may buy clothes or expensive toys such as bicycles for their grandchildren; father may help son with the deposit for a house or pay for a holiday.

It is therefore difficult to generalize about the structure and function of the family in the United Kingdom and it is equally dangerous to say that a nuclear family is inevitable in an industrialized society. In Japan many industries are so organized that they are compatible with an extended family network. All members of the family may be employed in the same firm which provides health and social services for its workers (in some cases schools and housing) and which may make provision for its old workers so that they are able to live in comfort and be cared for alongside their family for the rest of their lives. In this case industry has learned to 'fit' the family rather than the other way round.

NON-FAMILY GROUPS

In industrial societies there is an ever-increasing number of people living in non-family units (Table 2). These vary in character from single men and women living in a university hall, hostel, flat or bedsitter land possibly prior to marriage but with a family at the back of them even if geographically

Table 2. Percentage of people in Great Britain in private households in each age group who live alone.

	1973	1983	1984
Percentage of people aged:			
16–24	1.5	2.4	3.4
25–44	2.4	4.2	5.4
45–64	8.1	9.3	10.4
65–74	25.7	27.6	28.0
75 or over	40.0	46.6	46.6
All aged 16 or over	9.1	11.3	12.3
Percentage of males aged:			
65–74	13.1	15.3	15.8
75 or over	24.2	28.4	29.4
Percentage of females aged:			
65–74	35.8	36.8	37.4
75 or over	48.0	56.8	56.3

Source: General Household Survey.

distant, to the old or lonely, single, widowed, or divorced, who have no supportive family group. Obviously this latter group, unless involved in a career or job which provides both economic security and a degree of affection (may be shown as respect rather than love but either emphasizes the individual's worth), is in greater danger of feeling unwanted and unnecessary and has a high suicide rate.

Other non-family groups exist such as communes, religious orders, residential homes for handicapped or aged. Some of these will provide adequate substitute for families allowing division of responsibility, a sense of interdependence, security and affection, while others may emphasize the sinking of the individual in the common good.

Community

As with the family so it may be said that every individual belongs to a *community*. This may be identified as a geographical area but usually implies a degree of social coherence. A community has been defined as a 'constellation of institutions'. These include not merely formal and established social structures such as schools, churches, courts, business houses and settlements but also such phenomena as families, neighbourhood associations, political parties, gangs, clubs, newspapers and recreation centres (Wirth, 1938).

Industrialization has altered the structure of communities in much the same way as it has that of families. However, this means that throughout the world both pre- and post-industrial types may be found. The classical comparison between these two types of community was carried out by Tönnies, a German sociologist. He studied rural and urban areas and delineated two ideal-types which he called *Gemeinschaft* (community) and *Gesellschaft* (association). He described these as follows: in the 'community' people tended to live in extended families and had deep long-lasting patterns of interaction with their neighbours. They were frequently rural and lived off the land, being concerned only for their own life and that of their family and immediate friends. Attitudes and beliefs were largely folkways, traditional and new ideas were rejected. Conversely, in 'association' the families were more likely to be nuclear, social interaction superficial and transitory, life urban and industrial and the individual concerned with business and travel, being open to new ideas and knowledge and aware of the concerns of the world. These ideal-types are useful when studying the way people live. If information is required about individuals, then such factors as how they get a living, make a home, bring up their children, use leisure, adhere to religious practices and join clubs all help to indicate their attitudes and to what extent they show social coherence.

Durkheim, when discussing social facts, pointed out that ways of thinking and acting which exist outside the individual's consciousness have a coercive power on the individual and work to produce social solidarity and cohesion. When these 'outside factors' change and society's norms are not known the individual may develop a state of anomie.

Communities then are not just groups of people living together, indeed although all communities may be described as societies not all societies are communities. The word community implies having something in common. In the original use of the word and indeed as in the present 'commune' it means the sharing of goods, interests and values in a face-to-face situation. In a rural community each individual fills a multiplicity of roles and therefore there is a much greater intermeshing of life than in the town. The milkman may also be the church sidesman, captain of village cricket or a solo tenor in the local operatic society. He will probably be the son of a local farmer, married to the daughter of the licensee of the village pub and brother of the local school mistress. Patterns of interaction and reciprocity are therefore complex and compelling.

It is possible to distinguish three social areas which may be thought of as communities. The first is based on the locality in which the individual lives, such as village or parish; the second is based on occupation, providing it is one that requires a degree of interdependence in order to function — the fishing industry may be an example; thirdly there is one less clearly defined but made up of a friendship network. It is suggested that in rural communities these are more likely to overlap and in particular the friends are more likely to be held in common than in urban society.

Communities of all types frequently have some function in which they demonstrate their coherence. This may be the *manifest function* of raising money for charity but *latent function* will be an opportunity to demonstrate the 'togetherness'. The village fête may raise money for the restoration of the church but it also provides an opportunity for villagers to work together and to relax and enjoy themselves. A somewhat different type of community is that where the members have all things in common and maintain these groups by division of labour and sharing of skills. Some of these 'communes' have a religious function, for example convents and monasteries, while others have an ideological base, the best known example being the kibbutz. Many young people have reacted against the materialistic egoism of Western society and banded together in a shared life, some living off the land becoming completely self-sufficient.

Many types of institutional communities also exist. Some such as prisons are not entered voluntarily yet even here there develops a sense of interdependence amongst the inmates, and a common banding together against the staff.

Hospitals also may be seen as communities especially those catering for long-stay patients such as psychiatric hospitals or those for the mentally subnormal. Indeed in the eighteenth century many asylums developed from a 'mad doctor' taking a few guests in his own home. William Tuke, who founded the Retreat in York, saw himself as 'the father' of the 'family'. However, increasing demand, size and finance led to this personalized approach being abandoned and so the large hospitals developed. Within these large institutions patients became mainly dependent on the structure and the staff and there was little attempt to form a supportive group amongst the patients or to tolerate let alone give approval to individual differences.

In recent years there has been the development in some psychiatric hospitals of a move towards a supportive or *therapeutic community*. In these hospitals small groups of staff and patients live together in a democratic manner, decisions regarding activities being taken by the whole group. Individuals are encouraged to 'be themselves' and a wide range of behaviour that might be considered 'anti-social' is tolerated. The intense communalism involves sacrifices of privacy and confidentiality as confidences are shared and problems talked out. The emphasis is on communication, group-living and support and the goal of return to the larger community outside. In many ways it reflects life in a small village rather than the family life that Tuke aimed at in the Retreat, although it does not contain families within it but individuals.

The structure of the patient's family will have obvious implications for the nurse. The possibility or otherwise of care of a sick or aged person is affected both by the size of the dwelling occupied by the family (it is difficult to care for an ageing grandparent in a three-bedroomed, semi-detached house in company with growing children) and by the people available to carry out care. The expectation of many couples that both will be engaged in paid employment outside the home (indeed the only way in which many can buy their home is by the use of a joint wage) means that financial hardship is experienced if either has to stay at home to care for a sick parent or child.

The nurse working in an urban area is frequently appalled by the loneliness and lack of support that individuals receive from their neighbours when ill. Newspapers report people found dead after many months because no-one has missed them or people felt that 'it was not my business'. In a village this is less likely to happen, and although this interest may sometimes be felt as an intrusion by some individuals the mutual support received provides a sense of security should misfortune strike.

Although there is a tendency to feel that the extended family network and/or small community life is the best way of life, not everyone likes to live under the perpetual scrutiny of everyone else. Conflict in such a situation is more likely and often more intense because of the total involvement of the individual and the intermeshing of roles and may lead to bitter feuds. Also within many urban areas there may be communities which function more like rural communities than urban ones. Although a sharp distinction between the two is probably not realistic, the ideal-types may be helpful in measuring differences along a continuum and alerting health care staff to possible problems.

The ways in which the family copes with problems vary. Methods of coping with a handicapped child, for example, are those of 'passing' when the handicap is disguised both by the family and individual as much as possible; 'normalization' in which the handicap is dismissed as of little importance; and 'disassociation' which involves withdrawal from normal social involvement so that the handicap is not seen by other people. The reaction of families to the presence of a member whose prognosis is poor is similar, involving the continuum of responses from 'denial' of the likely outcome, despite information available, through 'anticipatory mourning' to 'acceptance'. Mental illness is particularly disruptive to a family, partly due to the *stigma* associated with the condition and partly due to the fact that it suggests an abnormality within the family. This has been highlighted by some work which implicates the family as the cause of illness (Laing and Esterson, 1964).

It is often within the context of the family that illness occurs and family responsibilities may affect whether or not help is sought to relieve symptoms. As a mother said when interviewed regarding her health: 'I wish I really knew what you meant about being sick. Sometimes I felt so bad I could curl up and die, but had to go on because the kids had to be taken care of . . . How could I be sick? How do you know when you're sick anyway? Some people can go to bed almost anytime with anything, but most of us can't be sick, even when we need to be' (Koos, 1954). Reaction of a family in the face of illness or handicap of one of its members may be a drawing together, an affirmation of solidarity. The disruption of normal family life that may result from the presence of one who is seriously ill or handicapped may impose strain on its members both emotionally, with regard to status, as may occur when a wife has to assume any of the functions of a father if her husband is ill or vice versa, and possibly financially, which the family as a socio-emotional unit is unable to sustain.

Laing has suggested that schizophrenic behaviour may be related to hostility, rigidity and mutual destructiveness within a family so that a child growing up within it has problems of identity and loyalty which eventually result in mental breakdown. Recent changes in society in relation to the role of the woman have raised questions relating to the child–mother relationship. Is 'mothering' an instinctive response to a child or does it have to be learnt? What effect does having a baby in hospital and therefore relating a normal function to illness have? Indeed does the concept of 'maternal deprivation' mean anything? Increase in incidence of child abuse makes these questions of vital importance.

All these are areas in which research is proceeding and which may yield interesting and helpful data on the part the family may play as the cause of illness.

References and Further Reading

Anderson. M. (1971) *Sociology of the Family*. Harmondsworth: Penguin.

Blythe. R. (1972) *Akenfield*. Harmondsworth: Penguin.

Bott. E. (1957) *Family and Social Network*. London: Tavistock.

Butterworth, E. & Weir, D. (1974) *The Sociology of Modern Britain*, Section 2. London: Fontana.

Fletcher, R. (1962) *The Family and Marriage*. Harmondsworth: Penguin.

Frankenberg. R. (1966) *Communities in Britain*. Harmondsworth: Pelican.

Jones, R.K. & Jones, P. (1975) *Sociology in Medicine*. London: The English Universities Press.

Koos, E. (1954) *The Health of Regionville*. New York: Columbia University Press.

Laing, R.D. (1969) *The Politics of the Family and Other Essays*. London: Tavistock.

Laing, R.D. & Esterson, A. (1964) *Sanity, Madness and the Family*. Harmondsworth: Penguin.

Oakley, A. (1976) The family, marriage and its relationship to illness. In Tuckett, D. (ed.) *An Introduction to Medical Sociology*. London: Tavistock.

Rappoport, R. (1960) *Community as Doctor*. London: Tavistock.

Robinson, D. (1973) *Patients, Practitioners and Medical Cure*. London: Heinemann Medical Books.

Rosser, C. & Harris, C.C. (1965) *The Family and Social Change*. London: Routledge & Kegan Paul.

Scotson, J. (1975) *Introducing Society*, Chapters 2 and 3, London: Routledge & Kegan Paul.

Shanas, E. *et al.* (1969) *Old People in Three Industrial Societies*. London: Routledge & Kegan Paul.

Tonnies, F. (1887) *Community and Associations* [translated by Lommis, P. (1955)]. London: Routledge & Kegan Paul.

Tuckett. D. (1976) *An Introduction to Medical Sociology.* London: Tavistock.

Tuckett, D. & Kaufert, J.M. (eds.) (1978) *Basic Readings in Medical Sociology.* London: Tavistock.

Tunstall, J. (1966) *Old and Alone.* London: Routledge & Kegan Paul.

Turner, C. (1969) *Family and Kinship in Modern Britain.* London: Routledge & Kegan Paul.

Wirth, L, (1938) Urbanism as a way of life. *American Journal of Sociology,* **XLIV**, 1–24.

Young, M. & Wilmott, P. (1969) *Family and Kinship in East London.* Harmondsworth: Pelican.

4 The Role of the Patient and the Nurse

Socialization has been defined as 'The process by which someone learns the ways of a given society or social group so that he can function within it.' (Elkin, 1960)

SOCIALIZATION

While a society may have laws which are written down and are therefore explicit it also has standards or norms, usually unwritten, which its members obey. Most people are able to call to mind some occasion when on entering a new society or group of people they have been told that 'it is not done' to say certain things, wear some type of dress, or behave in a manner which would be quite acceptable elsewhere. After a time, either as a result of kind instructions of an old member or by painful trial and error, the norms of the society are learned and the individual can be said to be 'socialized'. This sharing of meanings and expectations by individuals in a specific society enables a mental model of the world to be constructed and is one of the main considerations of the symbolic interactionist school of sociology.

A newborn child is in the same position. It has to learn what it means to be a male as opposed to a female, which activities please mother and which bring reproof, and what the sociologist, G.H. Mead, described as a 'consciousness of self'. This elementary learning which takes place initially in the home is one of the functions of the family described as *primary socialization*. Secondary socialization takes place in school, amongst friends or *peer groups*, in gangs or clubs, and later via the mass media. There is obviously an overlap in these two areas of socialization and some people draw the line slightly differently, using primary socialization to refer to that which occurs in childhood and secondary socialization to that which which occurs later. Socialization is not just maturation although both maturation and socialization normally occur together. Elkin describes some pre-conditions for socialization: first, an ongoing society for the child to live in. This may seem obvious but highlights the problems of either geographical or cultural isolation. A child who only interacts with his own family due to geographical isolation will have a lot to learn when he comes in contact with a wider group, as for example when starting school. The immigrant family striving to maintain its own culture in a totally different host society may lose the battle as the children mix with those socialized to a completely different way of life. Second, he specifies the requisite biological inheritance, that is, brain and intellect, and third, a 'human nature' by which he means the capacity to develop relationships and the capacity for empathy. Both these requirements may also seem obvious but they do emphasize the problem of socialization of the mentally handicapped.

ROLE

The part played by an individual as a result of being a male or female, or as a result of occupying some position in life, is described as a 'role' and may be expressed in the well-known quotation: 'All the world's a stage and all the men and women merely players', by Shakespeare. This demonstrates one aspect of role, that is, as part of a *social system*, a position existing and waiting to be filled. This position is already defined and has attached to it certain rights and privileges but also carries certain duties. In a family setting, a male is born into the role of son, brother, grandson and from an early age he learns what such roles involve in terms of behaviour as part of the socialization process. Such roles are part of the culture of any given society and society therefore produces the norms and values which structure how the role is occupied or played. In this case therefore role-playing, even for such basic roles as man or woman, has to be learnt, just as a play is already written but the actor has to learn his lines. This analogy tends to give the impression of rather rigid determinism, removing from the individual freedom of choice, however this is not so. Just as all actors are said to wish to play Hamlet, because they can place a different interpretation on the role, so also can an individual, even within the rights and duties laid down, pattern a role to himself or herself.

The other aspect of role is that while it may be part of a social system it is also the property of a person, and in this case the individual develops a picture of himself, both as he observes himself and as he perceives himself in the eyes of others. This situation has been described by two sociologists, Goffman and Mead, as 'the presentation of the self'. In this they say role definition for the 'I' (the objective part of the person) and the 'me' (the subjective aspect) take place by the way other people act to the individual. These other people may be classed as *significant others*, that is people who matter to the individual, or *generalized others*, that is the rest of society, and by the way they act and interact with the individual he gains a picture of himself and the way he should behave. Most individuals will have had the experience of curbing a desire to laugh because the people they are with obviously expect them to be serious. Parsons describes the effect of interaction on role-playing by saying that 'ego' (the individual) tends to behave as he knows 'alter' (other person) expects him to and equally 'alter' adapts his behaviour in anticipation of 'ego's' response. Such conformity is not however inevitable and when discrepancy occurs between expected and actual behaviour there will be embarrassment, conflict or tension in the relationship.

Some roles involve 'typification', that is, some varieties of action are considered appropriate for certain groups of individuals. An example of this is the type of behaviour expected by a nurse even when she is not involved actually in nursing. *Stereotyping* results when certain attributes of a specific role are exaggerated and generalized. Examples of this may be the portrayal of policemen as having big feet, doctors having charming bedside manners and nurses as angels of mercy (see page 140).

The process of socialization has been described in various ways. Social role theory suggests that as the individual matures physically and develops independence he patterns his behaviour on that of 'significant others' (parents, peers, people who have the greatest influence on an individual's evaluation of himself). As language develops the child is able to internalize the symbolism of the adult world; he is also able to assess and discuss with himself the experiences offered to him. A psychoanalytic theory based on the work of Freud traces the modification of instinctive desires under the activity of ego development, due to identification with the parent of the same sex and the *internalization* of the standards of both parents leading to the development of the super-ego.

Another theory, owing much to the work of Pavlov, is based on motor, mental and social training all aimed at 'tension reduction'. Reinforcement occurs as acceptable behaviour is rewarded and unacceptable behaviour punished.

As an agency of socialization the family plays a part both as an interacting structure in which the child learns not only his own role but also the roles occupied by his parents and siblings (playing at mummies and daddies is an acting out of the roles observed). Also as part of a community the family portrays other aspects such as racial norms or religious observance. School not only educates in terms of factual or abstract knowledge but also reinforces many of the things taught in the family (problems may arise when family and school values conflict) and also builds up status expectations by widening the horizons so that further development of the self is possible. The 'desire to belong' ensures that peer groups also play a part in the socialization process, dealing out rewards (acceptance) and sanctions (rejection) to enforce their specific norms. These norms may reflect those of the wider society but are often different and as such may produce a conflict situation for the child who may reject society in order to be accepted by peers. The mass media may reinforce any of the above norms or may be a source of conflict and change. It may also portray the norms, status positions and institutional functions of roles not experienced in other ways, for example the life of the policeman, the role of the nurse or doctor, the world of finance or industry. Naturally these portraits tend to be stylized and stereotyped which often results in disillusionment when the role is encountered in real life. This situation can often cause difficulty for the teenager choosing a career and may be one cause of wastage in a profession such as nursing if a glamorized version of the role has been perceived and thought to be real.

All individuals hold more than one status position and have many social relationships and therefore play many roles. These *multiple roles* (Figure 1) must be distinguished from what Merton (1949) describes as *role-set* (Figure 2). In this case the one role has many facets and areas of interaction. In both these situations (multiple roles and role-set) conflict may occur. A nurse as an occupant of a female role is not expected to help a strange man undress while as a nurse this

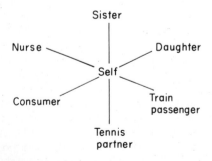

Figure 1. Multiple roles.

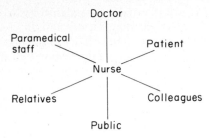

Figure 2. Role-set.

is perfectly acceptable. Further, as a nurse, interaction with patients may require an air of *authority*, while the doctor may expect a handmaiden. Occasionally there may be *role discrepancy* as when a first-year nurse may be thought to be qualified and a higher level of skill may be expected by a visiting doctor than she possesses.

Another problem is that an individual may deliberately disregard some aspect of his role. An example of this may be the charge nurse who cares for the patients but refuses to teach the student nurses. This is 'role deviance'.

Finally, some positions are on the boundary of more than one role and may make action difficult; for example, the staff nurse may wish to be associated with the students while being accorded the *prestige* of a trained nurse and the nursing officer may be seen as 'management' rather than as an expert in clinical care. As already indicated, many individuals and groups help define a role. The individual will first identify with a group to which she either belongs or to which she aspires, such as the new entrant to nursing aspires to be a registered nurse. The audience (in the nurse's case, the patients) will affect the way the role is played because of their expectations as a normative group the (already qualified) senior staff may lay down standards of behaviour, peers will interact in all areas of activity and there may be a comparative group, such as physiotherapists, with whom the nurse may compare herself.

Socialization is not normally a straightforward process. As already stated, people may view roles differently and hold varying values, resulting in conflict in the person being socialized. *Subculture* groups may develop within the larger culture; the multiplicity of roles played by any one individual may conflict as may their interaction in their role-set. Aspiration to other groups and roles may require changed behaviour. Finally, in a rapidly changing society, it may be difficult for the individual to 'keep up' with the changing norms, resulting in anomie.

Socialization is therefore a continuous process throughout life. As an adult the behaviour and expectations of others (generalized others) continue to affect the individual's view of himself. It is often a shock to a woman to realize people are perceiving her as 'old' and this may be resisted. Unfortunately, in that ageing is inevitable, the resistance may produce inappropriate behaviour, 'mutton dressed as lamb' or a pathetic attempt to be 'one of the girls'. Throughout the life cycle individuals change their physical and social status and also their self-identities.

One role of particular interest to people employed in health care is that of the patient. Illness and the inability to carry out normal activities are attributed to various agencies. In some parts of the world it is thought to be evidence of witchcraft, and in many, including the West, it may be seen as evidence of wrong-doing or an offence against God. Talcott Parsons described the adoption of the patient role in Western society in the following way: 'The illness must be outside the patient's control, the person must seek competent medical help, and must desire positively to get well but meanwhile will be excused all other roles. If these are complied with then the sickness will be considered fortuitous and blameless'.

Obviously such conditions may produce problems and discussion may ensue as to whether the results of drug addiction, or cancer of the lung due to smoking, are outside the patient's control. It may be difficult to define 'competent medical help' as many branches of fringe medicine such as osteopathy may bring relief, and of course it is sometimes difficult to decide whether the patient wishes to get well.

Suchman (1965) describes five stages of illness and medical care:

1. The symptom experiencing stage
2. The assumption of the sick-role stage
3. The medical care contact stage
4. The dependent patient role stage
5. The recovery or rehabilitation stage

This assumes a 'whole process' activity and although Suchman admitted that every stage might not be found in every case of illness, he felt that normally they would be present even in a condensed form. Such a scheme, however, focuses on the clinical condition with no account being taken of the social and/or cultural setting.

David Robinson (1971), studying families in Swansea in order to ascertain what factors were present in the process of becoming ill, asked these questions: What makes condition X an illness for A but not for B? What does it mean for A and B to be classed as 'an ill person'? He found many social factors to account for the variations. 'Tiredness' for example was rarely seen as a symptom of ill-health in a working-class man but might be considered so in a middle-class family. In another case both the sufferer and his wife would not allow the adoption of the sick role by the man because of a social factor — he was starting a new job. Indeed, all families studied indicated various manoeuvres which took place before the status 'sick' was confirmed and before medical aid was sought. The role of the significant other (wife, mother) in assessing the legitimacy of the claim to be sick and the dangers of being ill as against not being ill showed that evaluations were being made in both medical and social terms.

As Robinson points out, in the past, variations in perception of the validity of symptoms to be considered as illness have been focused on physiological factors. In view of his findings it would appear that social factors are of equal importance. In addition he demonstrates that often the patient role is voluntarily sacrificed or 'given as a gift', as in the case of a mother who could not 'go sick' because she was needed to care for her children.

The patient who reaches hospital has usually already assumed the status of a sick person but in the case of an emergency situation, such as a road accident, this has happened involuntarily with no prior evaluation of the pros and cons. Such a person, although in urgent need of medical aid, will often assert that he is all right; must get home because his wife will be worried; fret because he has the office keys; or become agitated because of social engagements that he will be unable to undertake. Doctors and nurses tend to become impatient with this attitude and frequently dismiss the objections as unrealistic, being concerned only with the clinical condition. However, such a person needs help to work through the factors that legitimize his status as a sick person so that he can be assured no blame is attached to his surrender of his normal social or occupational roles. This is often assisted by a visit of the significant other, such as his wife or boss, who says, 'Now don't worry, you just lie there and do what the doctors tell you so that you get better.' In rare cases the patient may assess the dangers of not having treatment against the dangers of surrendering other roles and decide that the social or occupational demands are more important. Such a patient may take his own discharge from hospital, an act which is almost always regarded as 'irrational' by medical and nursing staff.

Even the patient who has entered hospital after a period of treatment at home, or out-patient investigation, and has therefore had time to work through the implications of adopting the sick role may sometimes find that his original evaluation was faulty. Consider, for example, the patient who enters for what he considers is a minor thing — a funny black wart on his leg and finds that, because it is malignant, he has to have the leg amputated. The original adoption of

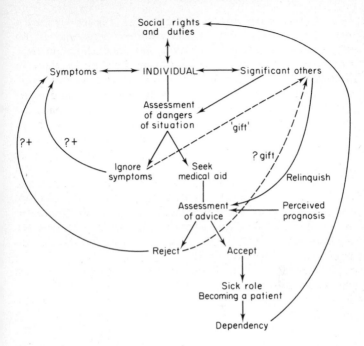

Figure 3. Steps in becoming a patient.

the sick role was on the understanding that it would be for a short time; reality shows that it will be for a long period, at the worst forever. Some social roles may never be able to be completely refilled and others must be abandoned entirely.

It certain cases the individual finds that the sick role provides an escape from social roles which were irksome, anxiety-producing, or beyond his capacity. Obviously such a person may be reluctant to forfeit the legitimate escape from these roles and will cling to the status 'sick'. The influence of the psyche on the soma is well documented but not always appreciated by the onlooker. Unfortunately non-clinical factors tend to receive scant attention by both doctors and nurses in their perception of the patient (Figure 4). Such a discussion does not mean that patients' behaviour is not affected by the clinical condition, but once again the areas of concern to the patient may not be the same as those of the staff caring for the person. Many patients are more concerned with the symptoms than with the underlying disease. While most doctors and nurses can understand a patient's preoccupation with pain or discomfort, many find it difficult to understand why some patients become distressed by rashes, bumps, scars, when they are either temporary or in places that do not show. The body, however, is an essential component of the self-image of the individual. 'All damage to the body is first and foremost damage to the self, therefore there is no really good treatment, no scientific treatment which does not take into account the primary necessity for healing and establishing the ego, for making the self-picture whole again.' (Stuart, 1953)

Definitions of 'illness' and the 'patient role' have within them the implicit assumption that this role is a temporary one and this therefore raises problems with regard to chronic disease or permanent disability. Robinson tells of a lady who when asked her condition stated that she was very healthy, this, despite the fact that she was waiting to be called into

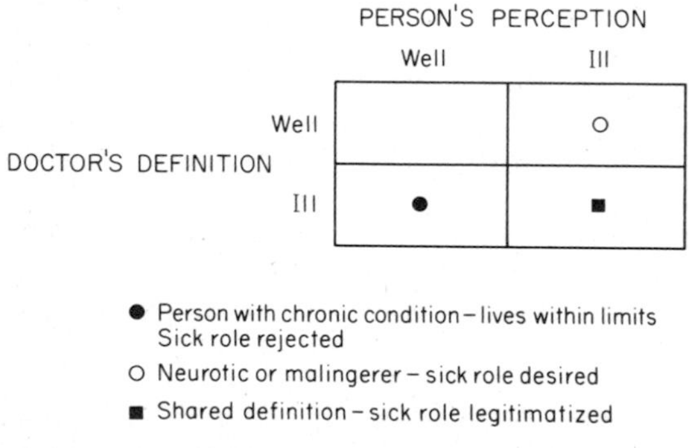

PERSON'S PERCEPTION

	Well	Ill
Well		O
Ill	●	■

DOCTOR'S DEFINITION

● Person with chronic condition – lives within limits
  Sick role rejected

O Neurotic or malingerer – sick role desired

■ Shared definition – sick role legitimatized

Figure 4. Health/illness assessment.

hospital for heart surgery. Often patients for routine surgery are described as entering hospital well but being discharged ill, completely ignoring the fact that if surgery was necessary then some disturbance in the body structure or function was present at the time of admission.

Mental illness is also frequently not seen as 'illness' in the traditional sense, hence the lack of sympathy often afforded to such sufferers. Words like 'depressed', 'anxious', 'tense', are used by people who consider themselves well and therefore there is reluctance to associate them with illness. Such patients are not encouraged to seek help and the patient role is only allowed grudgingly. Society may consider such conditions to be deviant so that the patient is told to 'pull himself together' rather than to seek medical aid. If illness is to be classified as deviance, it must be seen as behaviour which violates normative rules. However, no society expects its members never to fall ill or to occupy the status of a sick person and fill the patient role. On the contrary, illness is the expected occurrence of everyone's life, even those whose work is that of preventing, controlling or treating illness, or caring for the sick. It is difficult therefore to see how illness can itself be classified as deviant behaviour, even if the condition of the body may itself deviate from normal functioning. However, a sick person may behave in a deviant manner, that is, he may not seek competent help, he may not cooperate with treatment, he may in certain circumstances be deviant in not adopting the sick role, thereby spreading disease.

The closest link between illness and deviance is illness resulting from deviant behaviour, for example alcoholism, drug addiction, and, more recently appreciated, carcinoma of the lung. Such diseases may attract a certain amount of social disapproval because of the way in which they are acquired, but the illness itself cannot be classed as deviant. One is reminded of the armed services' approach to such conditions as sunburn which are classed as 'self-inflicted injury' and the unfortunate sufferer may find himself 'put on a charge' after treatment. Some behaviour exhibited by the mentally ill deviates from the social norms but again it cannot be said that the illness itself is deviant.

It has been said that the term 'sick' is much clearer to those who use it, namely the health practitioners and the researchers, than it is to those to whom it is applied, that is the patients.

The patient who eventually is admitted to hospital (unless in an emergency) has already progressed along the following path. Signs and symptoms have been recognized and their significance assessed. The standards by which these are judged are based on knowledge, factual from past experience or from hearsay. A conclusion has been reached as to the action most appropriate, that is, the dangers of seeking competent help as opposed to those of not seeking help or possible self-treatment have been assessed. Factors taken into account in the balancing activity are clinical, social and psychological and are weighted by past experience, knowledge and view of significant others. Once medical help has been sought there is once again an assessment of the value of following the advice given with the possible rejection or acceptance of the definition 'ill' or, if treatment is delayed as in the case of surgery for a hernia or varicose veins, 'potentially ill'. Once the patient has accepted the fact that he requires hospitalization there begins an anticipatory period during which activities are related to the future severance from social and occupational roles and to the adaptation of the patient role. This period is critical in developing the patient's expectations relating to the hospital, doctors, nurses and treatment. Naturally the patient tries to amass knowledge about his future role. This may be gleaned from official booklets issued by the hospital, from ex-patients, from fiction either written in articles in magazines or on television, and from magazine and television documentaries; from all these sources the patient builds up a picture of what will be expected of him and what he may expect. Past experience will also be recalled and even if not absolutely relevant will be used as a basis for the interpretation of new information. Efforts will also be made to 'set his house in order' and the way in which this is approached will be affected by the patient's assessment of the prognosis and time-scale of treatment. This period is characterized by uncertainty, both of future role and also of the time-span of each episode. Patients on a waiting list for admission rarely have accurate knowledge of when a bed will be vacant for them, which immediately puts them at a disadvantage and impresses on them that they are only one of many. No matter how urgent their clinical condition may seem to them, no matter how pressing social considerations may be (holiday dates, taking of examinations, business commitments), unless paying for the privilege, they cannot normally choose the time of their admission. Equally it may be almost impossible for them to discover the likely length of their hospitalization, convalescent period or date of resumption of work.

On admission the patient again attempts to define his situation with a mixture of uncertainty and expectations which may or may not be realistic. Anticipatory definitions are likely to have enduring social consequences, even if these definitions seem to an outside observer to be completely devoid of an 'objective truth' value. Problems are immediately caused where there is an absence of shared definitions between nurse and patient and this situation could often be avoided with more appropriate briefing of the person awaiting hospital admission. Indeed, socialization of the person into the role of patient does not commence at the point of admission but has been in progress from the moment the name was placed on the waiting list, admission procedures forming the *rites de passage*.

References and Further Reading

Anderson, E.R. (1974) *The Role of the Nurse*. RCN Research Project, **2**, 1. London: RCN.

Berger, P. (1966) *Invitation to Sociology*, Chapter 5. Harmondsworth: Pelican.

Butterworth, E. & Weir, D. (1974) *The Sociology of Modern Britain*, 2nd ed. London: Fontana. Readings in the section of socialization.

Coser, L.A. & Rosenberg, B. (eds) (1964) *Sociological Theory*, Section 8. New York: Macmillan.

Elkin, F. (1960) *The Child and Society*. New York: Random House.

Friedson, E. (1970) *Profession of Medicine*, Part III. New York: Dodd, Mead.

Mead, G.H. (1971) In Thompson, K. & Tunstall, J. (eds) *Sociological Perspectives*, 144. Harmondsworth: Penguin.

Merton, R.K. (1949) *Social Theory and Social Structure*. London: Glencoe Press.

Parsons, Talcott. (1966) On becoming a patient. In Folta, J.R. & Deck F. (eds) *A Sociological Framework for Patient Care*. New York: Wiley.

Robinson, D. (1971) *The Process of Becoming Ill*. London: Routledge & Kegan Paul.

Stuart, G. (1953) *The Private World of Pain*. London: Allen & Unwin.

Suchman, E.A. (1965) Stages of illness and medical care. *Journal of Health and Human Behaviour*. 5.

Tuckett, D. (1976) *An Introduction to Medical Sociology*, Section III. London: Tavistock.

Worsley, P. (1977) *Introducing Sociology*, Parts 2 and 6. Harmondsworth: Penguin.

Worsley, P. (ed.) (1977) *Modern Sociology. Introductory Readings*, Part 5, Section 36. Harmondsworth: Penguin.

5 The Hospital as an Organization

One of the major changes resulting from industrialization is that our total life experience such as education, occupation, leisure activities, health care, and so on, takes place in an organized fashion rather than haphazardly. Even friendship groups which are not normally considered organizations may have their own type of structure: there are shared beliefs and feelings, someone may be the person who initiates action, another the life and soul of the party and another the person who is acknowledged the brains of the group. However, such groups are not organizations in the formal sense as although they possess a form of structure, norms and may have a specific goal they do not possess any formal decision-making machinery and no explicit rules for regulating members' behaviour.

An organization, then, is defined as a formal structure directed to the achievement of a specific goal or goals, with a hierarchy of administrative officials, and rules and regulations to control its activities.

A classical model of an organization, a *bureaucracy*, was first described by Max Weber (1920). This description he said was an ideal-type of organization, not necessarily the best but one which would result if all the concepts used to describe organizations were carried to their logical conclusion. He delineated two main characteristics of bureaucracy: division of labour and a hierarchical structure of management. In the hierarchy each official has a specific job description and knows precisely his area of responsibility, whom he controls and equally to whom he must report and be accountable. Thus in a bureaucratic organization the formal communication channels are up and down (though many would say mainly down) from the board of directors via the manager, supervisors, foremen, chargehands to the men on the shop floor.

Nearer home, in the health service, both the structures advocated for nursing administration by the Report of the Committee on Senior Nursing Staff Structures (Salmon Report) (Figure 5) and that of the reorganized Health Service (Figure 6) show the typical structure of a bureaucracy as

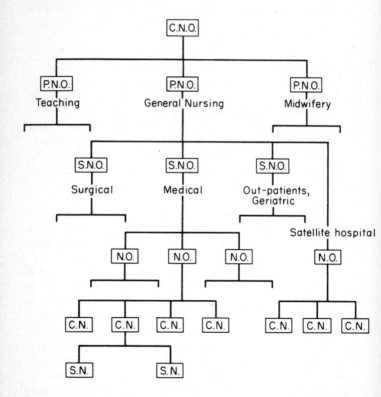

Figure 5. A nursing management 'pyramid'. *Source*: Salmon Report (Committee on Senior Nursing Staff Structures, 1966).

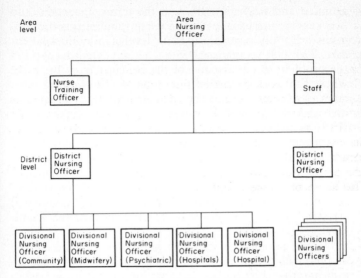

Figure 6. Nursing area with districts. *Source*: Management Arrangements for the Reorganized National Health Service in Wales 1972.

described by Weber, who felt that this was the most rational and efficient form of organization. He based his arguments of efficiency on the fact that tasks are distributed rationally, each official knows his duties and his actions are governed by formal rules, therefore he does not act in an arbitrary fashion; actions of officials are coordinated and continuity is ensured as any qualified person can take over any specific post and knows what he should do.

However, while such a structure may be efficient in an organization, such as the army, in many situations it is too rigid, the rules (often described as red tape) do not allow personal discretion and do not easily adapt to change. Adherence to the job description may result in timidity and in some cases secrecy as each individual guards his job from others. The length of the communication network frequently leads to lack of understanding and confidence between management and workers. Although the terms 'managers' and 'workers'are not usually used in the hospital setting the criticisms still apply, particularly at the level of individual patient care. The 1981 reorganization to a certain extent recognized the problem of the distance of the manager from the place where the work is carried out. One level of control (area team) was removed and the management team situated at district and unit level. However, following the report of Mr Griffiths on management in the NHS, the concept of consensus management by a team of equals — nurse, doctor and administrator — has given way to that of management by one person, at district level, called the 'general manager'. The same principle applies at unit level. It is too soon to comment on whether this type of management structure will effectively solve the problems of efficiency in the health service.

Despite popular belief that it is the doctors who are the all-powerful figures in the hospital, a good deal of evidence indicates that they are largely at the mercy of the ward sister. A wide range of medical, paramedical, domestic, administrative and other staff have contact at different times with the patient; the ward sister is the one who provides the continuity, she assumes control over 'her' territory and 'her' patients. Within the organization the sister serves as a communication system relaying information between the transitory specialists who may never meet and interpreting their decisions into instructions and task allocations and also giving understandable explanations to the patients. Because of this, 'getting on well with sister' is an essential component of success.

The communication network of a typical ward sister is shown in Figure 7 and confirms that one of her main roles is that of coordinator of a vast range of people and services, all of which have as their focus the patient. The Report of the Committee on Nursing (Briggs Report) (1972) showed 258 movements in and out of a male medical ward between 09.43 and 15.45 hours. Obviously, to enable this function to be carried out effectively the ward sister must be able to

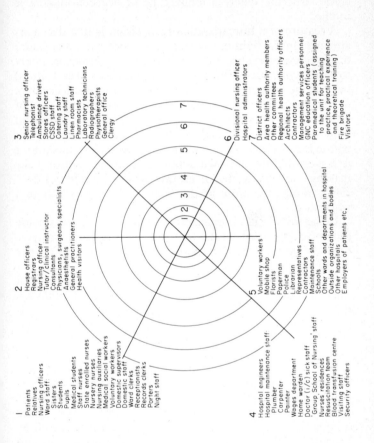

Figure 7. Communication network of a ward sister.

make 'on the spot' decisions relating to priorities, access, techniques, information dispersal and so on. This type of activity is in direct contrast to that produced by a bureaucratic structure where a longer line of decision-making is implied.

A feature of a bureaucratic organization is that decisions are made in the light of carefully developed rules which aim to cover every eventuality. Patient care is, however, likely to be idiosyncratic in character and nurses (as well as doctors) need to be prepared to function in a state of uncertainty. Trying to cover every situation with appropriate rules of action is not feasible. On the contrary, ward sisters and nurses at the bedside need to have freedom of movement within a broad policy framework. Legally, each trained nurse is responsible for her own actions and no amount of 'rule-making' can absolve her from this personal burden of decision-making, therefore at the bedside bureaucracy cannot work.

Using this classical organization model, a study was made of the behaviour of workers on the shop floor. It was postulated that payment by results and a reduction in fatigue would result in an increase in output. As a result of this work, time and motion studies were carried out to find out the most efficient way of producing specific goods and then the workers were paid by results, that is 'piece-work'. This method is still used in many organizations including hospitals and is the way in which productivity bonus schemes are operated.

However, the idea that men worked entirely for profit was disputed and a famous piece of research at the Hawthorne Works of the General Electric Company in the United States showed that workers did not work as hard as they could despite the possibility of a production bonus (discussed by Brown, 1954). It was also found that changes in lighting and hence possible changes in fatigue produced greater output whether the level of illumination was increased or decreased. These somewhat strange findings stimulated further investigations and the researchers found that employees formed groupings at work which affected their level of performance and that they responded to non-economic factors as well as rewards. For example, a worker was more anxious to be liked by his informal work group than to achieve a bonus by exceeding the group's norm of output (so called 'rate-busting'), equally not reaching it (chiselling) would also result in disapproval by the group. In each case sanctions, that is punishment, were likely to be employed by the group, taking the form of loss of respect and affection. This recognition of the importance of human relations in industry also demonstrated the importance of the leadership by foremen and supervisors and the need for effective communications at all levels of production. It is likely that if the reasons for action and the results of decisions are explained to workers, then less conflict will result and the organizational goals will be more readily achieved.

Obviously not all organizations are industrial and not all produce goods. The organization of a hospital or a university cannot really be compared with that of a car factory. The goals of a prison or a boarding school are not the same as those of the civil service or a petroleum plant yet they are all organizations. Common factors are goals, although these will vary widely, and all have a decision-making and communication system which coordinates activities. As the result of some empirical studies, Burns and Stalker (1961) have divided organizational structures into two main types. The first they call 'mechanical'; these accord to the classical model with a hierarchical structure and long lines of communication. The second are described as 'organic' structures and in the communications and authority are lateral rather than vertical and there is a greater sense of interdependence. Generally speaking the mechanical model is suitable for stable organizations where goals are fixed and there is little prospect of change and the organic model for organizations where there needs to be a high degree of flexibility and where change is common. A hospital ward or a social work agency are organizations that probably need an organic structure in that goals, needs and actions may vary daily.

One of the problems in any organization is that of power. Weber divided authority, which he described as legitimated power, into three types. The first he said was *'Charismatic'*, related to the personality of the ruler; the second *'Traditional'* and therefore legitimated by custom; and the third *'Rational'*, legitimated by rules which were accepted as necessary for goal achievement. While it is possible for all types to exist in present-day organizations, obviously the commonest type is the latter, rational power legitimated by rules (*'Legal/Rational'*).

However, another sociologist, Etzioni (1964), has shown that such a distinction may be adequate to explain social relationships but is not an adequate explanation for complex organizations. Instead to achieve control a system of formally distributed rewards and sanctions is needed. The means of control may be categorized as physical or coercive as in prisons; material or remunerative as in factories; and symbolic or normative as in voluntary institutions, for example convents (see page 64). Obviously the type of power exerted will affect the way people comply with the control and will relate to the commitment of the individual to the institution. This is shown briefly in Table 3. To a certain extent compliance may be ensured by the method of recruitment to the organization. Fairly obviously, normative institutions need to be more rigorous in their selection than coercive struc-

Table 3. Power, compliance and organization.

Power	Type of compliance	Type of organization
Coercive	Alienative	Prison, custodial mental hospital
Remunerative	Calculative	Factory or other economic organization
Normative	Moral	Voluntary organization, therapeutic community

tures. Certainly there is evidence to show that the more rigorous the selection the more the successful individual will be committed to the goals of the institution and on the whole there is a tendency towards congruence in that individuals seek organizations that 'suit them'.

People may obey orders because they have agreed to abide by the rules or obedience may be related to the 'acceptability' of the order in that it lies within the range that in a general way was anticipated at the time of undertaking a connection with the organization. This immediately suggests the possible areas of conflict and frustration that may arise for individual nurses (and indeed patients) in hospital organization if their 'anticipatory definition of the situation' was different from the actual situation. The nurse who anticipates her function as one of interpersonal relationship, supporting the patient emotionally while carrying out intimate physical care, will inevitably question the legitimacy of orders that stress personal non-involvement and task orientation and may also reject the role of health educator. Equally, the patient who expects to be considered as an individual will be resentful of commands which ignore his idiosyncrasies.

Despite the apparent conflict between the mechanical model, which suggests a pyramid, and the organic which may imply a wheel with spokes representing the lines of communication with the decision-maker at the hub, hospitals share many of the basic tenets. As far as nursing is concerned bureaucracy in the form of a pyramid exists from the top down to the ward level. Here it tends to stop and the picture changes to that of a wheel with the ward sister as the centre of a complex communication network. In this latter model hierarchy or even legitimacy is not important; instead rational self-interest provides the motivation which in the case of the nurse will result in an endeavour to meet both the patients' and her own goals.

All types of organization have to ensure the socialization of their workers (or inmates) into the organization's goals. This may be done formally by induction or in-service courses or informally as the new entrant gradually learns the norms.

Goals obviously vary according to the organization, some are run for the benefit of their members, some for profit for the owner, some are service organizations in that the client is the main beneficiary (schools, hospitals) and others may be for the public at large as in the case of the army.

In some organizations where a large number of professional workers are employed there may be conflict between the organization's administrative authority and professional autonomy. The dichotomy is shown in Table 4. Organizations may get over this conflict by 'buying-in' professional knowledge from outside, thus they can exert control by specifying the boundaries within which the professional may work. Others act as 'service' organizations, that is they provide the structure in which professionals can work. This might be said to be the case of a hospital, although even in this situation conflict can occur as the administrators have goals of efficiency and cost-effectiveness which may clash with the professionals' goal of cure, care and research.

Table 4. Administrative and professional authority.

Administrative authority	Professional authority
Power hierarchy	No hierarchy
Power transferable	Power individual
Ultimate justification of an act is:	Ultimate justification for an act is:
1. It is in line with the rules	1. The individual thinks it is right (professional judgement)
2. It is approved by a superior	2. Support by peers of professional judgement

SOCIALIZATION OF THE PATIENT INTO THE HOSPITAL

It has been pointed out that it is important for roles to be synchronized. A doctor cannot act as a doctor unless the patient acts like a patient. However, there are no courses in how to become a patient and little in the mass media which portrays the role realistically. Some education may be given via women's magazines or the *Family Doctor* booklets but of necessity these can only reach a very limited audience. It is hard for staff, whose working life is spent in a hospital, to appreciate the bewilderment felt by most patients as they enter this totally alien environment with its peculiar smell, glimpses of frightening apparatus, hurried efficiency and impersonal approach. Many patients describe their entrance to hospital in terms of 'being placed on a conveyor belt', 'felt the whole experience was unreal', 'felt I was outside watching what was happening'. Such reactions indicate the profound sense of disorientation produced in individuals who up until that time were confident both of themselves as individuals and of the various roles they had to play: *alienation*, or powerlessness in the extreme. This sense of loss of identity is often increased by the inevitable admission procedure. Despite efforts made by senior staff to ensure that patients are received on wards in an individualized manner, the need to produce a method by which the patient can be rapidly identified, records commenced, departments notified and treatment initiated, results in a standardized routine practice in which the patient may well feel like a package being processed to ensure it reaches its required destination.

The process has been described as a series of steps: separation (from the old life), transition (no-man's land) and incorporation (into a new status). The fact remains that whatever terms are used and despite the universality and necessity of the procedure the point of admission is the first formalized contact with a person that the patient has in this new and potentially terrifying environment. This means that the attitude of that person sets the standards by which many subsequent events are measured and interpreted.

The strangeness of the situation is further enhanced by the words used, such as next-of-kin, which may indicate to the patient that the condition is more serious than he thought, and the knowledge required, for example the National Insurance number, may not be known. These terms, common enough to the staff but outside a lay person's vocabulary, may produce a state of confusion and feeling of worthlessness. One patient said, 'I couldn't answer all the questions: they won't think I'm incapable, will they?' The very efficiency of the nurse may be interpreted as lack of warmth and prevent the patient asking questions that would help to alleviate many of the anxieties inherent in the situation, and the assumption that the hospital information booklet will deal with these problems is optimistic in the extreme. The patient therefore frequently concludes that either he is worse than he thought or alternatively that someone with such a trivial complaint should not be taking up the nurses' valuable time, and that although his absence from family and work may be important to those affected, his presence in hospital is important to no-one.

Reaction to this situation, which may be felt as abandonment by the outside world of family and friends, is frequently similar to that exhibited by bereavement: initially one of shock and a sense of unreality, the patient may exhibit an air of self-confidence and even jocularity, denying that anything is wrong and claiming that the stay in hospital will be very short. This stage is then replaced by a feeling of sadness, hopelessness and helplessness often accompanied by a sense of guilt at 'not keeping well' or of anger against the circumstances that have produced the illness. Such a patient may be quiet and withdrawn and not participate in the chat of the ward. As in mourning, this stage is frequently accompanied by physical symptoms such as insomnia, loss of appetite, indigestion, constipation and headaches. Finally there is a gradual acceptance of the situation as socialization into the ward and hospital community occurs. This progress of adaptation has been frequently commented upon when the hospitalization of children is discussed but it also occurs in adults. Goffman describes this process as alienation, modification and re-birth, that is, a new way of conceiving self.

One of the problems associated with rapid turnover of patients in acute wards is that there may be insufficient time for this process to be worked through and the patient is discharged with a sense of unhappiness and frustration.

The appreciation of self is determined by individual self-awareness and secondly by a 'seeing oneself through the eyes of others'. The child learns therefore to distinguish between 'I' the subject and 'me' the object. The realization of other people's perspective of 'me' is assisted by the ability to 'take on their role' and therefore see through their eyes (this is the perception of self by 'the generalized other'). However, the new inmate of a hospital may have insufficient knowledge about the roles of the doctor, nurse and other health workers to be able to do this and therefore the patient grasps at symbols such as language and gestures which may assist this understanding. The fact that words may have a different and specific meaning in a clinical setting and actions which would be regarded as a physical assault outside hospital may be freely used by staff to patients (for example intimate physical examination) make this reorientation of self a long and painful business. Even as a child is unable to define that situation in ways differently to those around him who have already defined it and laid down the rules of conduct, so the patient finds himself forced into the view of himself that is held by the staff and other patients on the ward. This lack of understanding makes the patient particularly vulnerable to non-rational beliefs and practices which may even result in his exploitation. Actions which have already had 'meaning' attached to them outside the hospital may be eagerly seized upon by the patient and given the same interpretation, for example the first cup of tea, especially if given on arrival, may be seen in terms of hospitality and acceptance even if it is merely a chance occurrence, tea being routinely served at that time. A routine bath may be considered to imply that the patient is 'dirty' and being 'put to bed' may recall nursery punishment.

Staff in hospitals and particularly nurses consider that their attitude to patients is one of interest and that they do things for the best and mean to be kind. However, it is essential to find out how the individual defines the situation, 'If men define situations as real they are real in their consequences', and there is no guarantee that the perception of nurses' actions will be seen in the terms of the nurses' intended consequences.

SMALL GROUPS

Although the size and structure of wards vary greatly it is fair to say that most of them operate within the factors or laws that are used to describe 'small groups'. Definitions as to what constitutes a small group vary. A primary group is usually described as individuals in a situation where all can have a face-to-face relationship, where each person receives a distinct enough impression of each of the others to be able, at a later date, to give an account of them as a person. Most writers consider that primary groups must be small, actual numbers stated vary but are usually below ten. However, the degree of permanence and frequency of interaction are also important. In this context the ward can be seen as a 'primary' or 'small' group. This results in individual patients developing a feeling of 'belonging' in the ward. To achieve this there are certain standards of behaviour considered acceptable or unacceptable and one of the first things the newcomer to the ward has to learn is this code of behaviour. Although a few of these may be in writing in a hospital information booklet, most are informal and conveyed to the newcomer by the 'old' inhabitants. The norms will vary with each group and therefore over a period of time may change even though the ward's size, structure and function remain the same. The sort of behaviour that may be regulated in this way will probably include decisions over ventilation, smoking (when not regulated by strict hospital ruling), when general talk is appropriate and when quiet is appreciated, the way in which the more mobile can assist the bedfast by making the early morning tea, arranging flowers and running errands. Even more subtly it will probably include standards of behaviour relating to expressions of pain, grumbling about conditions and bantering with staff. Patients tend to achieve conformity to these norms both by direct verbal information and comment and by such attitudes as facial expressions, dropping hints, talking over the offence and, when deviance appears intractable and offensive, by ostracizing the individual so that while still 'in' the ward he is not 'of' it. Such people are often classed as 'unpopular' by the other patients.

As with other groups, roles develop in the ward: the oldest, the youngest, the most ill, the most active and so on. Each of these positions in the group will confer on the holder certain rights; for example, the youngest may be allowed to make more fuss or receive extra attention but these rights will also carry with them duties; the youngest, if mobile, may be expected to fetch and carry for the others. Leaders will also arise in the ward. There may be an *instrumental* leader, that is one who organizes and gets things done, and an *expressive* leader, one who is able to make personal contact with individuals, to comfort or encourage them and provide a listening ear.

Obviously this group activity performs an important function in the life of the individual. All patients in a ward have had to relinquish membership of the small groups to which they belonged outside, and therefore are deprived of the sense of security provided by the norms and roles which make up part of the image and performance of 'the self'. This they can to a certain extent regain in the ward group. In long-stay institutions there are dangers in this substitution of the institutional community for the outside community. An extreme example of socialization occurs in what Goffman (1961) has described as *total institutions*. These are organizations that pervade the whole life of the individual such as religious institutions like monasteries, prisons, long-stay hospitals and the armed services. In these cases the new entrant is subjected to procedures which are aimed at stripping aspects of his previous personality prior to replacing them by one 'functional' for the organization. For example, in the hospital the patient is admitted and given a number, his clothes are removed and may be replaced by institutional clothing, his previous activities such as smoking or drinking may be curtailed. He will have to get up and go to bed when ordered and any tendency not to conform to the daily routine will result in *sanctions* being imposed by staff. These sanctions may be excessive adherence to rules and removal of small privileges or the ignoring of requests. An excellent account of life in a long stay hospital can be found in Thomas Mann's 'The Magic Mountain'.

Patients certainly 'feel the power' of the hospital and may comply in any of the three congruent ways indicated (Table 5). Although the 'patient role' paradigm would imply that involvement should be normative/moral in character, it is true that many patients feel that they 'ought' to obey when in hospital because 'that's what they came for' and the hospital staff must know best. Others, possibly but not necessarily, more intelligent or better informed, may query some of the orders that they receive and discover that sanctions can be applied to discourage 'non-cooperation'. Stockwell (1972) found that nurses used techniques like 'forgetting requests', not talking to patients, refusing gifts and favours, enforcing rules, and sarcasm as methods of indicating disapproval of patient's actions and attitudes and as a means of achieving cooperation. Equally, 'good' behaviour could be rewarded by nurses by giving the patient more time, allowing per-

Table 5. Congruent power/compliance patterns (see page 56).

| Power | Involvement (compliance) | | |
	Alienative	Calculative	Moral
Coercive	1	2	3
Remunerative	4	5	6
Normative	7	8	9

sonalized interaction or lapses in rules and by a willingness to accept small gifts. Patients who reacted to such sanctions by 'cooperation' were operating under a remunerative/calculative pattern of involvement or in extreme cases one which was coercive/alienative. If long-stay patients they would be likely to be the group whom Goffman (1961) identified as able to 'work the system', apparently obeying the rules but in practice avoiding them. Much of this type of activity is a direct attempt by patients, especially those in long-stay institutions, to maintain their identity. Bureaucracy tries to ignore personal identity, seeing only 'role identity'. Health care in contrast is considered to be care concerned with 'the individual' and the two systems are likely to be incompatible.

COMMUNICATION

Despite the security provided by the ward unit and the pressure of organization, patients rarely forget that they 'belong' to the outside world. To sustain this sense of 'temporariness' and to assist in his understanding of the situation the patient tries to establish a timetable of events; first, of the day, when meals occur, doctors visit, relatives allowed in and the like and then the likely length of his stay. This timetabling consists of the patient picking up cues that he considers relevant to his own condition from the progress of other patients, statements from staff, stories related by visitors and so on. The doctor's tone of voice, the way the nurses smile, the frequency of radiographic examination, changes in drugs, are all considered significant and used as milestones along a path the length of which is not known and the destination uncertain. The resilience of the patient is shown by his adjusting this timetable when key dates or occurrences do not develop as predicted.

Despite increased education the majority of people still have little knowledge of the working of their own bodies (Boyle, 1970) and regard much medical treatment as magic. This situation is not helped by the attitude of some medical personnel who appear unable to explain either conditions or treatment in simple terms but by the use of technical language preserve the atmosphere of mystique. Some of this inability to communicate is related to class difference. Most medical staff are middle class in origin and do not know the words working-class people use to describe parts of their bodies and normal functions. Others make a great effort to enable the patient to understand but because of the feeling of inferiority that many patients possess they are unable or unwilling to ask questions or to indicate that they have not understood what has been said and therefore they remain confused and in ignorance. A patient commenting on this said, 'In general, I don't think I have been told very much. Probably it's my own fault really. There is a reluctance actually to do anything positive with the doctors and nurses, unless they are really pushed. I guess there is no real reason why they should go out of their way to tell me all about myself.' While this may be the view of one patient, most feel that they have a right to know about themselves and may see the nurse as the informer or interpreter in their quest for information, perhaps because she is often of the same class as the patient, perhaps because the patient has observed that she treats all the patients alike or perhaps because she is there for a longer period of time and in particular is available at night when most patients' fears and anxieties are expressed. Studies show that it is a frequent occurrence for the patient to say, 'I didn't understand the doctor, can you tell me?' Unfortunately not all nurses respond to this role of interpreter but refer the patient back to the doctor; this may be due to ignorance of what has been said or to fear of overstepping their area of responsibility, or a complete insensitivity to the situation, especially where the question is not asked directly but tied up in other conversation or behaviour. There is little doubt that some of the confusion exhibited by patients, especially the elderly, could be prevented if more information was given and time taken to ensure that its meaning and implications were understood. Anxiety frequently acts as a barrier to understanding and has been shown by Hayward (1975) and Boore (1978) to retard recovery.

The way in which patients interpret the position of their bed in a ward and the significance they attach to it being moved is often not appreciated by the ward staff. It is customary in many hospitals to move the seriously ill and/or dying either into a side-room or into a bed in the corner of a ward. The reasons for this are obvious: the patient is more easily observed and there may be more room around the bed for equipment and staff to carry out care. However, this practice is not universal and patients may be placed in a corner bed for other reasons, but unless these are adequately explained they will frequently interpret the position as one indicating the seriousness of their condition. Occasionally the system is even more cruel than intended and there are accounts of patients who, having watched a succession of patients being moved into the corner prior to dying, have experienced great mental stress and occasionally physical collapse when moved there themselves.

A study of preoperative preparation of patients revealed wide discrepancies in the understanding by patients of the instruction not to eat for a specified time prior to anaesthetic. Many patients had little idea why they were not allowed to eat, the commonest reason given by them was it was 'to stop them being sick' and one patient who thought this was unlikely anyway ate his way through a pound of sweets! Another felt that 'nil by mouth' only referred to food and continued to drink. This non-adherence to instructions was not helped by the fact that nurses and doctors did not always agree on the procedure to be followed and therefore conflicting instructions could be issued. Although a great deal is often said and written about lack of understanding on the part of the patient which implies that it is related to lack of knowledge or intelligence, it frequently occurs that the knowledgeable and intelligent patient is also left in the dark. Staff assume that such a patient will automatically know what is happening, why treatment is given and what is expected when in fact this is not the situation. It is commonplace to

assert that 'a little knowledge is a dangerous thing' but sometimes 'a lot is even worse' and anxiety may be increased
because of understanding of possible complications, potential dangers or long-term implications.

The non-verbal aspect of communication has received considerable attention in the last decade and the interpretation
of such symbols as a smile, a tone, or a raised voice, is
something that is learned by the very young. Many a baby
has cooed at a soft voice when the words being said were
anything but soothing, and alternatively cried bitterly if
Mother's voice has been raised and angry even though the
anger and words are not directed at him. So with the patient:
the rapid efficient tones of the nurse admitting a patient
may make him feel he is a nuisance. Nurses have become
so imbued with the idea that they are always short-staffed
and therefore always busy that even if the pace does slacken
they still carry with them the air of 'bustling efficiency'
which the patient often interprets as 'don't bother me, I'm
busy'. Although traditionally the nurse is the person who
'soothes fevered brows' many are now apparently afraid of
touching patients. This may be a reflection of British culture
which tends to frown on physical contact other than a stiff
handshake between strangers. Patients, however, both
expect and appreciate the hand on the shoulder or the hand
being held during periods of stress, either physical or mental.
There is an 'aloneness' experienced by patients in sickness
and if both sick and away from home, physical contact with
another human being reassures them that although the
experience cannot necessarily be actually shared, nevertheless the situation is understood by another and that they care.

Patients' reactions to uniform can also vary. Many find
the traditional uniform with stiff white apron and cap reassuring, seeing it as a symbol of competence and therefore
producing a sense of trust and confidence in the wearer,
even though she may be the most junior member of staff.
Others find that the uniform acts as a barrier and are pleas-
antly surprised if the nurse is met off duty to find she is
'just an ordinary girl like my daughter'. Some feel that the

uniform enables intimate care to be given without embarrassment because the nurse in uniform is seen as something
ageless, sexless and impersonal, while others resent this very
fact and regard the uniform as a weapon of power. The
variety of uniforms in any institution may increase the sense
of confusion the patient feels and may lead to embarrassment
when status is wrongly guessed, particularly as the present
'national' uniform is similar to that worn by a variety of
shop and domestic workers!

Patients frequently regress in behaviour when ill to a
childlike, dependent state and some of this regression may
be due to the way they perceive some nurses treat them like
children. The role of the patient in a ward is often like that
of a child in a school. He is expected to 'keep his locker
tidy', to 'eat up his dinner' and any deviation from prescribed
routine is considered 'naughty'. Much has been written
about the part the maternal instinct plays in nursing and it
has been suggested that only by seeing the patients as children can the nurse feel compassion for them and be able to
carry out unpleasant and intimate tasks. The incongruity of
an eighteen-year-old acting in this capacity to an older man
may be unbearable and many patients turn with relief to the
often middle-aged auxiliary in whom 'motherliness' is a
natural attribute.

A sense of dignity is important and contributes to human
happiness so it is obviously distressing to the patient who
feels that it is being debased. The use of surname only, for
example 'Jones' rather than 'Mr Jones', may produce this
feeling, or the old lady called 'Gran' instead of 'Mrs Brown',
a title of which she has been proud for many years. This
may be due to thoughtlessness or even an attempt to be
friendly but can produce the feeling of a school or prison
rather than that of a hotel or home where the nurse is the
hostess.

Most inquiries indicate that the patient perceives the situation in hospital as one over which he has little or no control
and that is potentially threatening to him as a person. Some
institutions are beginning to realize the effect of architectural

and organizational structure on this perception and are attempting to replace long corridors and wards with smaller more intimate structures to enable the easier formation of primary groups. In the same way the value of team nursing and patient allocation as opposed to task-orientated care is being appreciated so that patients and staff may be able to form face-to-face groups with the result that a therapeutic environment will become a reality with the mutual identification and sympathy engendered.

References and Further Reading

Abrahamson, M. (ed.) (1967) *The Professional in the Organisation*. New York: Rand McNally.

Argyris, C. (1964) *Integrating the Individual and the Organisation*. New York: Wiley.

Blau, P. (1956) *Bureaucracy in Modern Society*. New York: Random House.

Boore, J. (1978) *A Prescription for Recovery*. London: RCN.

Boyle, C.M. (1970) Differences between Patients and Doctors' Interpretation of some Common Medical Terms. *British Medical Journal*, ii, 286–289.

Brown, J.A.C. (1954) *The Social Psychology of Industry*. Harmondsworth: Penguin.

Burns, T. & Stalker, G.M. (1961) *The Management of Innovation*. London: Tavistock.

Committee on Senior Nursing Staff Structures (1966) *Salmon Report. Report of the Committee on Senior Nursing Staff Structures*. London: HMSO.

Dales, E. & Michelon, L.C. (1966) *Modern Management Methods*. Harmondsworth: Pelican.

Etzioni, A. (1964) *Modern Organisations*. Englewood Cliffs, NJ: Prentice-Hall.

Etzioni, A. (1969) *The Semi-Professions and their Organisation*. New York: Free Press.

Faulkner, A. (1985) *Nursing: A Creative Approach*. London: Baillière Tindall.

Goffman, E. (1961) *Asylums*. Harmondsworth: Penguin.

Hayward, J. (1975) *Information — A Prescription Against Pain*. London: RCN.

Hunter, T.D. (1967) Hierarchy or arena, re administrative complications of a socio-therapeutic regimen. In Freeman, J. & Ferndale, P. (eds). *New Aspects of the Mental Health Service.* Oxford: Pergamon.

Jones, R.K. & Jones, P. (1975) *Sociology in Medicine.* London: English Universities Press.

Katz, D. & Kahn, R.L. (1966) *The Social Psychology of Organizations.* New York: Wiley.

Lipton, D. (1970) *Management and the Social Sciences.* Harmondsworth: Penguin.

Management Arrangements for the Reorganized National Health Service in Wales 1972. Welsh Office.

Mann, T. (1924) *The Magic Mountain* [translated by Lowe-Porter, H.T.]. London: Nationwide Book Service.

Scott, W.R. (1966) Professionals in bureaucracy: areas of conflict. In Volmer, H. (ed.) *Professionalization.* Englewood Cliffs, NJ: Prentice-Hall.

Silverman, D. (1970) *The Theory of Organizations.* London: Heinemann.

Stockwell, F. (1972) *The Unpopular Patient,* RCN Research Project, **1**, 2. London: RCN.

Tuckett, D. (1976) *An Introduction to Medical Sociology,* Chapter 17. London: Tavistock.

Weber, M. (1920) *The Theory of Social and Economic Organizations* [translated by Parsons, T. (1964)]. New York: Free Press.

Wilson-Barnett, J. (1983) *Nursing Research: Ten Studies in Patient Care.* London: J. Wiley.

Wilson-Barnett, J. & Fordham, M. (1982) *Recovery from Illness.* London: J. Wiley.

Worsley, P. (ed.) (1970) *Modern Sociology. Introductory Readings,* Part 6, Harmondsworth: Penguin.

6 Work and Life-styles

Interest in the occupation of an individual is universal. It is a question on every form and an opening gambit in many conversations between strangers. Introductions frequently state name and then job: 'Mr Brown, meet Mr Jones, he works in advertising. Mr Brown is a dentist.' The reason for this is that unless the occupation is very esoteric it will convey quite a lot of information about the person: level of education, social class, possible income, likely interests, voting behaviour and many other facts. Of course there is a problem in defining what work is — ask any housewife or man who has just dug his garden — but generally it means activity undertaken for money.

The work that people do has changed over the years both in its content and form of organization: from agriculture as the prime occupation to the production of artefacts by industrial methods: and from coercion in slavery or feudalism to freer involvement in a career. While many feel there is still a form of coercion in work, there is little in our present society that actually forces an adult to have an occupation. Nevertheless there is a moral feeling that 'work is good'. According to Weber (1920), this feeling developed in the sixteenth century when the puritans postulated a link between hard work, thrift and religious salvation (this was in contrast to the previous Christian condemnation of wealth and usury). This *protestant ethic* is said by Weber to have engendered the 'spirit of capitalism' and ensured that money was available for the new machines and factories required in the Industrial Revolution. As riches were therefore perceived as the reward of hard work, poverty was condemned as an indication, not of holiness as previously, but of sloth. Furthermore the evolutionary ideas of Darwin and the survival of the fittest spread to the social scene and therefore the successful and rich were seen as the fittest to own and direct the new industries, the entrepreneurs or capitalists.

The importance of this *ideology* is that it affected the attitudes demonstrated by the owners of industry to their workers and legitimized many of the abuses of the early factory systems. It was these abuses that led to some of the work of Karl Marx. He argued that increasing division of labour and mechanization removed the need for intelligence and skill in work and furthermore any one individual could no longer exert any control over the work process or see the result of his labours in the form of production of a total article. Marx said this removed all sense of purpose and satisfaction from work, producing a sense of alienation. What is more, because the worker does not own what he produces he has nothing to sell but his labour. Profits produced by the worker (member of the *proletariat*) therefore do not belong to him but to the factory owner, the capitalist (one of the *bourgeoisie*). If work is the basis of society (*infrastructure*), alterations in its organization will alter all other aspects of society (*suprastructure*) and this relationship between work and society will be discussed later.

Marx was talking about a factory system of work and today would no doubt apply his theory to workers on assembly-line systems such as car workers. However, there are other forms of organization of work in industry, one of these is called a sociotechnical system. Studies show that the way work is organized affects the satisfaction that a worker gets from his work. The aspects of alienation have been described as 'powerlessness', that is the inability to control the work process, management decisions or conditions of employment; 'meaninglessness' in that no sense of purpose can be seen in the relationship between the individual task and the overall product; 'isolation', due to the absence of informal work groupings and impersonal administration; and 'self-estrangement' in that the work does not allow self-expression. Work therefore becomes purely *instrumental*, that is, it is undertaken purely for the sake of money rather than for *expressive* reasons such as self-fulfilment. Assembly-line workers are likely to experience all these conditions while workers employed in the making of high-class handmade furniture escape in that they have a reasonable degree of control over their work, are able to complete most if not all of an article, work in a small factory and work group and may be able to obtain intrinsic satisfaction from the completed article. Because some researchers attribute the level of industrial unrest in occupations such as the car industry as due to alienation, some factories are trying to allow their workers to work in small groups rather than on an impersonal assembly line, and to let them complete more if not all of the total product. This is the move to what is described as 'job-enrichment'.

The feeling that there is a sense of dignity bestowed on a person who is employed is demonstrated by the anger and despair of the unemployed, in some cases, erupting in street violence. This is not just due to lack of money as in the UK Social Service payments prevent starvation. One person in seven is unemployed in the UK (1985) and there are signs that this may result in increased illness and death.

Even when employed, there are hazards at work. The 1972 Robens Report on Health and Safety at Work pointed out that every year about half a million people suffer injury at work and that a total of 23 million working days are lost annually on account of industrial injury and disease. Doctors and nurses working in industry consider that many of these lost days are preventable.

PROFESSIONALS IN HEALTH CARE

Word association, a technique employed by some psychologists on the basis of some party games, links together concepts commonly occurring together. If the word 'patient' is said to most people, they immediately say either doctor or nurse. Perhaps it is not surprising as doctors are the people who frequently define a person as a patient and nurses make up the largest group of employees in the health care team. Both these occupational roles are frequently defined as *professional* and although the term profession is applied to many occupations there is no universal agreement as to the definition. However, it is generally agreed that to be considered as a profession an occupation must have a body of knowledge which is then used as a basis for the practice of a specific skill. There are clearly defined conditions of entry to education and training and there is an examination at the end of the period of education before the appropriate qualification is awarded. Professional organizations control the type of education and standard of examination leading to the professional qualification, and most have a code of ethics backed by a disciplinary procedure to control the activities of their members and protect the client.

Originally the professional person, such as a doctor or lawyer, sold his skills direct to a client for a fee and where this still happens the professional can be said to exercise complete control (via his professional body) over his activities. However, many professionals are now employed either by the Government, as in the case of doctors in the National Health Service, or by industry where for example many organizations employ their own lawyers. Nevertheless, the professional in these situations still has a high degree of autonomy of action.

The possession of a special area of knowledge, not easily acquired by the layman, tends to produce an aura of 'mystique' around many professionals and this gives them a high status in the eyes of the public and may be useful in achieving control over the client but may also be abused. The high status achieved by such professions as medicine and the law has encouraged many other occupations to seek recognition as a 'profession', and so a heterogeneous collection of activities is now awarded this status. The variations are tremendous for while all may have a body of knowledge tested by examination, some are client orientated and have a high degree of autonomy, for example architects, others are employees and indeed could not easily exist in private practice, for example teachers or social workers. Nurses fall into this latter category and while they have a professional organization, The Royal College of Nursing, different statutory bodies, the National Boards for Nursing, Midwifery and Health Visiting, control examinations, while the United Kingdom Central Council for Nursing, Midwifery and Health Visiting keeps the records of practitioners and exerts disciplinary action. It is doubtful whether a specific body of knowledge called nursing exists, though a similar criticism could be made of medicine. In both cases knowledge from the biological, behavioural and natural sciences is used to develop a specific skill. In the case of the doctor the specific skill is medical diagnosis and treatment, in the case of the nurse it is the assessment of nursing need and delivery of patient care. Both groups, however, have high public esteem and are considered to possess knowledge not easily accessible to the ordinary man. Most doctors and nurses are employees of the National Health Service and, as with other professionals employed by similar agencies, there is often the problem of conflict of interests. Professional goals may not be those of the organization. Service agencies such as teaching, social work and nursing are classed by some writers as semi-professions due to their lack of autonomy, absence of a specific area of knowledge and practice which may be carried out at a simple level by the layman.

The 'professionalization of everybody' is largely an attempt to achieve public esteem and to justify higher remuneration. Possibly it would be more helpful if the emphasis were placed on professional attitudes such as understanding and ethical conduct towards the client without undue thought for the monetary reward. Indeed, one of the interesting factors about work of a professional nature is that hours of work are not strictly adhered to and it tends to permeate leisure activities so that there is no sharp demarcation line between work and pleasure and the professional's friends are likely to be fellow professionals. This is in contrast to the manual worker whose leisure is usually a complete withdrawal from his working activities.

LIFE-STYLE

The distinction made between manual workers (sometimes described as 'blue-collar'), non-manual workers such as clerks, managers (white-collar) and professionals such as doctors and lawyers, implies more than just a description of the type of work done. Occupational classification is reflected in the way the individual lives, leisure pursuits, the way in which children are brought up and educated, political affiliation, and even life expectancy and pattern of disease. This *life-style* is classified and, as 'social class', is a tool used to describe the cluster of attributes that may be attached to any specific individual.

Despite assertions by political parties, religious leaders, governments or bills of rights that all men are equal, it is obvious to any unbiased observer that society does not treat them as such and what is more has usually produced some rational argument for inequality. The way in which the strata in society are ordered can be based on a group's objective possessions such as the level of money, or it may be measured by the position that man occupies in terms of occupation or status, or it may be related to power either possessed or available. Finally it may be a subjective decision related to the position that the individual feels he occupies. Some of these methods of measurement are based on the assumption that a person's occupation will also affect his or her level of income. However, many professionals earn less than members of manual occupations, their advantage being that they usually can exert greater power in society. Although class is external to man it is also something which he himself has defined; it is both an objective and a subjective reality.

It is impossible to consider the concept of social class without the name of Karl Marx coming to mind. As discussed earlier in this chapter, the division of labour, the ownership or non-ownership of the means of production produces a supra- or subordinate position among men and this is the foundation (or infrastructure) on which the rest of society, legal and political forms, and all other types of social organization (the suprastructure) rests. Social class, by Marx's definition, relates to groups of people who are in the same relationship to the means of production; the bourgeoisie as 'the haves' and the proletariat as 'the have-nots' and these he felt were irreconcilably opposed. The basis for this opposition he claimed was due to the exploitation of the worker by the owner in that the worker produced more money than he received in terms of wages. This excess value over and above the wages he contracted to work for, increased the owner's capital, widening the gap between him and his workers. As a result of this increasing gap between owners and workers or, to use Marx's terms, bourgeoisie and proletariat, he anticipated overt class conflict, revolution and eventually a class-free society.

The commonest objective measurement of social class is the Registrar General's Social Class Scale used since 1911. This is based on occupational grouping (Table 6). Some of these groupings may now appear inappropriate as changes in technology have resulted in some heavy manual jobs becoming light and unskilled in that all that may be required is button pushing.

Income, both size and how received, is closely linked with occupation and therefore may be used as a social-class scale although some professional groupings such as the clergy may occupy a low place on the income rating while high on that of Registrar General's Office Classification.

The Hall–Jones scale is based on occupational prestige, which may or may not correspond to income level on the Registrar's scale and has seven rather than five points on the scale. (The Registrar's scale has classes 3, 4 subdivided into non-manual and manual.)

Subjectively, people may be asked to which social class they 'think' they belong. This is difficult to standardize as people frequently name the class to which they aspire and this may be reflected in their life-style — speech, manner of dress and possessions.

Despite the fact that the scales used to measure social class are divided differently, the ordinary person usually

Table 6. An example of social class based on occupations as defined in the Registrar General's Office Classification of Occupations.

Social class	Occupation
Non-manual	
1. Professional	Doctors, dentists, university teachers, chemists, physical and biological scientists, clergy, barristers, solicitors, architects
2. Intermediate	Managers, local authority senior officers, nurses, pharmacists, dispensers, teachers, journalists, laboratory assistants, technicians, ships officers, aircraft pilots, executive officers (civil service)
3. Skilled	Typists, secretaries, clerks, cashiers, office machine operators, other local authority and civil service, police, draughtsmen, commercial travellers, shop assistants
4. Semiskilled	Street vendors, telephone operators, barmen/maids, waiters, waitresses, maids, valets
Manual	
3. Skilled	Florists, coalface workers, smiths, radio and radar mechanics, electricians, sheet metal workers, tool-makers, fitters, plumbers, engine and bus drivers, firemen, hairdressers
4. Semiskilled manual	Agricultural workers, furnace-men, surface coal miners, machine operators, boilermen, storekeepers, roundsmen, bus conductors, postmen
5. Unskilled manual	Labourers, messengers, railway porters, charwomen, office cleaners, window cleaners, lorry drivers' mates, kitchen hands

thinks in terms of three social classes, upper, middle and working class, and each of these has a stereotyped set of characteristics attached to it. Common examples of these characteristics are those frequently used on television to convey the social class of a specific character such as the 'cloth cap' image for the working class or the 'chinless wonder' of the upper class. People themselves may or may not identify with their social class, that is they may or may not have a degree of *class consciousness*. However, there is still evidence to show that the social class to which a person belongs may shape his life experience and affect his attitudes and values.

CLASS VARIATIONS IN FAMILY LIFE

There are marked variations related to social class in the way families behave and bring up their children. For example, more middle-class mothers breast-feed their babies than do those of the working class who tend to 'overfeed' their infants with proprietary feeds by adding excess sugar. This use of sweet foods (and later sweets themselves) is often a working-class way of demonstrating affection which appears less easily verbalized than in the middle class. It has been shown (Bernstein, 1958, 1971) that the way mothers speak to their children is different. The working-class mother tends to issue commands such as, 'come here', 'shut up', 'don't', with few sentences containing verbs and with little or no explanation. The middle-class mother is more likely to say, 'I'd rather you made less noise dear', or 'I shouldn't touch the fire because it may burn you.' This differentiation in the way in which the child is talked to affects the vocabulary developed by the child, the ability to express thoughts and eventually the skill in using abstract concepts. The use of words such as 'rather' or 'less' indicate that the child is learning to make comparisons, is able to pick up social cues and is sensitive to the fact that disobedience will bring further disapproval or even punishment. The working-class child learns to respond to imperative language and may miss cues in the extended or elaborated language of the middle class. The working-class child is conditioned to a more direct, descriptive, concrete type of language with emphasis on the emotive rather than on logical implications. This is called a public language. Quality and strength in this form of communication are conveyed by non-verbal means, such as tone of voice or facial expression. The middle-class child is able to use both types of language whereas the working-class child may have to interpret 'formal' into 'public' language before it is understood.

The effect that this early exposure to language has on eventual ability to benefit from education is important, as is the fact that the working-class home may contain fewer books than that of a middle-class family. Even the provision of toys will vary with class, the working class tending towards expensive and often unsuitable toys while the middle-class parent goes for 'educational' toys. The working class child often has more pocket money than the middle class child and this giving of money either directly or in kind may again be a way of showing affection which the middle class show more with words and interpersonal relationships.

There are also class differences in the relationship between husband and wife. In the middle class the equality of the partners means greater independence for the wife while in the working class it means more shared interests with the man who spends less time in clubs. It has been said that: 'Lower-class males concede verbally fewer rights than women obtain and upper-class males concede verbally more rights than they grant!'

When it comes to the case of the aged, the working-class children visit their parents more frequently and give physical help, perhaps because they are more likely to live in the same neighbourhood. The middle-class children visit less but frequently provide financial help.

SOCIAL CLASS AND EDUCATION

The relationship of social class to education is an important one in that education tends to be a determinant of occupation and life-style. Education is one method of socialization and is part of the process whereby *culture* is passed from one generation to another. The word culture in sociology is often misunderstood. In everyday use it is thought to mean such things as art, music and literature but as C.P. Snow in a famous lecture pointed out, in the industrial world it should probably also include science and technology. Certainly it is unreasonable for present society to value highly the creative aspects of life and not to appreciate man's achievements in using and, to a certain extent, mastering nature. However, when sociologists use the word they mean it to include all aspects of life of a specific society. This will include art, music, literature, technology, political and religious beliefs. The family will assist in passing on some of their knowledge and beliefs, but much of it is purveyed by the educational system along with possible preparation for an occupational role.

Until the nineteenth century universities saw their role as that of preserver and purveyor of culture in the original sense. Indeed, technology has only been accepted as worthy of academic study in very recent years and it is still considered rather doubtful academically in some universities, as are subjects which are vocational in character, although recent government pressure linked with financial constraints are rapidly altering this view. The struggle nursing has had, and indeed is undergoing, to be considered suitable for inclusion in university programmes is partly due to this resistance to knowledge which is 'job orientated'.

Initially occupational skills were passed on by the master to his apprentice, textbooks were unnecessary and teaching took place 'on the job'. With the advance in technology and increasing division of labour this type of teaching became less suitable and although still retained in some of the crafts such as carpentry, more of the teaching now takes place in institutions. Indeed technical colleges developed in response to the need for such teaching, although practice may still be 'on the job' in sandwich courses or day-release apprenticeship schemes.

Another factor is that more occupations require a qualification which is gained by examination. This is particularly so for professionals, many of whom cannot practice without a statutory qualification (compare nursing since the 1919 Nurses Registration Act). This has meant more formal selection of entrants to an occupation, for if qualification is to be gained by success in examination, then selection must ensure that the entrant has the ability to take examinations even if the skill gained is a manual one! This link between educational progress and society's perception of need is important and continues to this day.

Historically, educational systems in the United Kingdom were by class for class. With the coming of the industrial revolution the upper class began to realize their reliance on the workers and to see the need for educating the working class, and therefore from 1830 onwards general education was imposed on the working class from above. (Contrast the United States where education is a community project.) This fear felt by the upper class of the new workers was expressed in the 1870 'Forster' Education Act which first made education compulsory in order to 'gentle the masses' and following the increased franchise to 'educate our masters'. From the beginning there developed a three-tier system related to social class. The upper class went to public schools and Oxbridge, the middle class to grammar schools and some universities (many of the redbrick universities were founded by members of the middle class) and the working class had the opportunity of three years of secondary education as the school-leaving age remained at fourteen years until after the Second World War; only a few reached university (Table 7).

By the beginning of the twentieth century the 'by class for class' concept was replaced by an élite system. Selection for further education took place via examinations and some scholarships became available for the children of poor parents. However, few working-class children achieved, even if they aspired to, further education and this situation continued until the 1944 Education Act which had, as its aim, education that would be comprehensive, according to age, aptitude and ability. Despite this aim, inequalities have per-

Table 7. University graduates by social class of fathers (at time of graduates' entry to university): observed rates as a percentage.

Social class	Male	Female
I	12	15
II	34	39
III non-manual	14	13
III manual	19	14
IV	6	5
V	1	–
Unknown	14	12

Source: Derived from Census 1961. Socioeconomic Group Tables 1966.

sisted and are still largely related to social class. It is still possible for those with money to buy their children's education and it is probable that the standard of private education is superior to that provided by the State in terms of pupil–teacher ratios. It may be technically superior and certainly it is able to transmit social skills and 'know how' that are prized by many employers and the established professions. They also, by use of an extended 'old boy' network, may secure entrance for their pupils into desired positions.

Comprehensive education, which was the aim of the 1944 Act, has been slow to develop and is still not universal throughout the United Kingdom despite pressure from Labour governments. By eliminating selection via the 11-plus examination and having schools of children with mixed ability, it is hoped that there will be equality of opportunity for all children regardless of factors such as social class. This could also increase the chances of social mobility and could alter the pattern of society. Unfortunately recent research shows that these aims have not been achieved.

The British educational system and its effect on social

mobility have been contrasted with those prevailing in the United States by Turner (1964). He described the British system as one of 'sponsored elites' in which potential recruits to *élite* positions (top jobs, professions, government) were selected early (11-plus examination or similar) and sent to élite schools, hence to top streams within these schools and via Oxbridge to the positions at the top of the status ladder. By contrast, the United States has a 'contest' system. Education is open and available to all, there is no selection, and it continues until the individual drops out of the race at his level of ability. In the United Kingdom the emphasis has been on selection of the most able, in the United States it is on motivation so that all individuals are allowed to continue education until they achieve their highest potential (see paragraph 159 of the recommendations of the Briggs Report on a common portal of entry to nursing which reflects a similar ideology).

In the United States, therefore, there is less emphasis placed on knowledge for its own sake and more on vocational courses. As already suggested, society's structure, and particularly the origin of its élites, affects the type of education system that it supports.

Even now in the United Kingdom state comprehensive system the fact that many teachers hold middle-class values and attitudes may result in them reacting against working-class children, defining them as stupid, aggressive and unambitious. The working-class child may start with the disadvantage of a restricted language pattern, a home with few or no books and a lack of family expectation of educational success, all of which add up to a picture of educational deprivation at the primary stage which is difficult to overcome.

Once classed as 'slow' or 'stupid' there is a tendency for this definition to act as a *self-fulfilling prophecy*. Teachers act in such a way that the child eventually accepts their definition of his lack of ability, motivation to improve falls and the child fails to achieve its potential. This 'cycle of deprivation' in education is further increased by the fact that the most able teachers frequently teach the most able pupils while the less able get the inexperienced or unsuccessful teacher or suffer from frequent staff changes.

The Robbins Report (Ministry of Education, 1963) commented on the pool of ability untapped in the working class and there is little doubt that, despite comprehensive schools, the education system still tends to support the *stratification* pattern of society (see Table 7) and is unable to modify the differences in values and expectations that are brought into the schools by the pupils. In a class-differentiated society, class is an aspect of culture and education is a process by which the specific culture is assimilated. Even entrants to Open University courses reflect a similar class bias (see Table 8).

Table 8. The 1971 intake by Open University to social class of students and students' fathers: observed rates as a percentage.

Social class	Students	Students' fathers
I	20	8
II	62	26
III non-manual	11	13
III manual	5	34
IV	1	13
V	0	4

Source: Derived from Table 6. McIntosh & Woodley (1974).

YOUTH SUBCULTURE

Of course some working-class children rise above these disadvantages but they face other difficulties due to the conflict of norms that may exist between school with its emphasis on work and educational achievement and their peer group which may hold quite different values. It is difficult for a child to fulfil homework requirements in a flat or house that is small and noisy, and with a peer group that values going out and about in the evenings. Taunts of 'swot' or 'bighead' are not easy to bear. Even more difficult is the determination to stay at school if ex-school mates are earning good wages in local factories. The present high level of unemployment amongst school leavers has encouraged more to stay on at school to obtain further academic qualifications such as extra 'O' or 'A' level certificates, others take advantage of youth opportunity schemes. However, the level of frustration is proportionally increased when, despite these qualifications, no job is forthcoming.

A study of eighty working-class grammar school boys carried out in 1962 showed that when forced to choose between the value of the school and those of the home, the boy usually withdrew to the support of his peers and rejected the attitudes of the school. In fact, the researchers found that the only boys of working-class background who succeeded at grammar school were those whose families had middle-class connections such as a mother who came from the middle class.

The part played by peer groups in the socialization of the young is very important. Youth groupings act to bridge the gap between childhood and adult life. The teenager tends to feel that he belongs to neither the world of the child, which is secure and non-demanding, nor to the world of the adult, where he may be recognized as an individual. Peers help to provide the security still required and also ascribe status which is still withheld by the adult world. However, this solidarity can only be achieved by adhering to the group norms which tends to emphasize activities, dress, methods of speech and common experience. In an effort to achieve the identity offered by the peer group the adolescent will reject both parental and school attitudes if they clash. This type of behaviour is usually described as youth culture and is seen as a subculture of the main society. On the whole it is related only to the peer-group activity and does not impinge on the general attitudes of society. The union of peer groups and working-class values and attitudes tends to be antagonistic to the values of educational institutions such as ambition, hard work and scholastic attainment. Middle-class youth groupings show higher regard for scholastic achievement and a greater evidence of ambition and willingness to postpone the gratification of earning money, although the period of high youth unemployment which has affected those with advanced educational qualifications has modified these attitudes.

The way in which the teacher perceives his or her role and the goals of the school will also affect the pupil. Due to the statutory school-leaving age of sixteen years and the fact that many children wish to leave before then, many teachers find themselves in a custodial role, keeping children at school and out of mischief. This attitude is likely to get a response of aggression from the pupils who may perceive the teachers as having a lack of interest in them as individuals. Such schools will be likely to have a high truancy rate. This is in contrast to the school and teachers who maintain academic goals, desiring to motivate pupils and assist them to reach their highest potential. Such schools have lower truancy rates, less delinquent behaviour and lower staff turnover.

GOVERNMENT POLICY

The political philosophy of the country and, in particular, its government will obviously affect the type of educational system provided. For example, a government committed to the abolition of class differences will provide equal opportunity in education and may in fact discriminate positively so that children from culturally deprived areas get extra facilities. This type of provision was suggested in the Plowden Report (1967) which highlighted the fate of children in depressed areas of cities: poor home conditions, out-of-date school buildings, rapid turnover of teachers and so on. Economic needs of the country also exert pressure on the type of education provided. A country that needs more doctors will ensure places for them in medical schools and put more money at their disposal in the form of grants while cutting down places available for students to read classics. In times of economic recession, education may be one of the areas to be severely affected. Greater emphasis tends to be put on vocational courses and those without an obvious contribution to the needs of society are squeezed out, as has occurred with the cuts inflicted on universities in the last decade. The effect of such action on the cultural life of the country is not immediately apparent and may be difficult to measure. Perhaps it is worth remembering that 'man does not live by bread alone'. Society may well suffer from the lack of indefinable civilising effect of those non-productive subjects.

SOCIAL CLASS AND ATTITUDES

Traditionally manual workers live in relatively stable close-knit communities. Self-help and neighbourliness are valued highly and there is a reluctance to leave home even if it results in 'bettering oneself'. Children get expensive toys, and holidays such as Christmas are saved for throughout the year and then celebrated with a big show. Cleanliness, care-fulness (in terms of money), 'keeping oneself to oneself', self-respect, are all virtues which are emphasized and there is a 'them' and 'us' approach to members of the middle or upper class.

More of the working class vote Labour, believing that the political parties are linked with class interests. Research has shown that members of the working class who do not vote for the Labour Party tend to aspire to and identify themselves with the middle class. Members of the middle class are more likely to vote Conservative, be geographically mobile, have friends outside their home network and tend to take part in more outside activities and associations. In particular they are often the organizers of community projects such as play groups for under-five year olds, drama societies and tennis clubs. A comparison between working- and middle-class perspectives can be seen in Table 9.

Table 9. Working-class and middle-class perspectives.

	Working-class perspective	Middle-class perspective
General beliefs	The social order is divided into 'us' and 'them': those who do not have authority and those who do	The social order is a hierarchy of differentially rewarded positions: a ladder containing many rungs
	The division between 'us' and 'them' is virtually fixed, at least from the point of view of one man's life chances	It is possible for individuals to move from one level of the hierarchy to another
	What happens to you depends a lot on luck; otherwise you have to learn to put up with things	Those who have ability and initiative can overcome obstacles and create their own opportunities. Where a man ends up depends on what he makes of himself
General values	'We' ought to stick together and get what we can as a group. You may as well enjoy yourself while you can instead of trying to make yourself 'a cut above the rest'	Every man ought to make the most of his own capabilities and be responsible for his own welfare. You cannot expect to get anywhere in the world if you squander your time and money. 'Getting on' means making sacrifices
Attitudes on more specific issues	(on the best job for a son) 'A trade in his hands'. 'A good steady job'	'As good as start as you can give him'. 'A job that leads somewhere'

Table 9. —*contd*.

Working-class perspective	Middle-class perspective
(towards people needing assistance) 'They have been unlucky' 'They never had a chance' 'It could happen to any of us	'Many of them had the same opportunities as others who have managed well enough'. 'They are a burden on those who are trying to help themselves'
(on trade unions) 'Trade unions are the only means workers have of protecting themselves and of improving their standard of living'	Trade unions have too much power in the country'. 'The unions put the interests of a section before the interests of the nation as a whole'

Source: Goldthorpe & Lockwood (1970)

SOCIAL CLASS AND STATUS AND POWER

A somewhat different view of social stratification was held by Max Weber. Although he also considered that social class was closely related to economic power and that property or lack of it was the basis of all class situations he argued that absolute or *relative deprivation* would produce solidarity which would lead to action directed to social change and that the real crux of the situation was social honour or status. This concept of status highlights a different aspect of society because while it is true that it may be tied to class and wealth, it may also be related to occupations or professions which may be highly placed on an occupational scale, yet be comparatively poorly paid. One of the most obvious examples of this is the clergy. At another level status may be afforded by social-class associations such as working-men's clubs or trade unions. Status may in fact be *ascribed*, that is, related to some aspect of birth, or may be *achieved* by personal effort such as passing examinations.

Power in society is also frequently related to social class. This power may be seen as the ability of one individual to impose his will on another despite the other's resistance. The development of power is linked with the possession of goods or facilities that another requires and is based on an individual's 'exchange capacity'. If one person has more of any desired factor than another, then a power situation develops as the one with the most to offer can, if his demands are not met, withdraw facilities. Power may be likened to money as a symbolic but generalized system of exchange which has become acceptable in a society due to socialization and is therefore related to a surplus of resources. In a primitive society goods are distributed according to need but in a complex society a surplus accumulates which endows the owner of the surplus with power.

Traditionally the working classes have endeavoured to achieve power by joining trade unions (Figure 8), although their membership is at present declining.

SOCIAL CLASS AND HEALTH

The effect of social class on health and illness commences from the moment of birth. Infant mortality figures for Scotland (those for England and Wales are likely to be similar) shown in Table 10 indicate that the baby born into a working-class home is more likely to die before birth or in the first weeks of life and this disadvantage continues throughout life (Table 11). Table 12 describes the use of health services by children up to the age of seven. This gradient continues in later life (Table 13) in persons reporting illness.

There is also a difference in the types of illness experienced by the varying classes (Figure 9). The reasons for these variations may be fairly easy to see in some cases; for example, the standard of living, diet, lack of exercise or smoking may be precipitating factors in the development of some diseases such as coronary heart disease. At one time these were linked with middle-class executives, but this group has

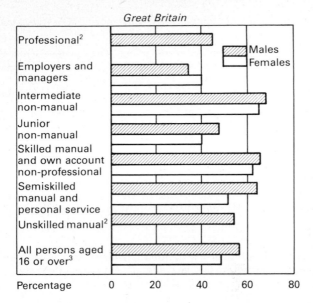

Great Britain

Professional[2]
Employers and managers
Intermediate non-manual
Junior non-manual
Skilled manual and own account non-professional
Semiskilled manual and personal service
Unskilled manual[2]
All persons aged 16 or over[3]

Males
Females

Percentage   0   20   40   60   80

[1]Full-time employees only.
[2]Data for females are not given as they relate only to a small number of employees.
[3]Excludes armed forces and people who have never worked.

Figure 8. Trade union membership: by age and socioeconomic group, 1983. *Source*: General Household Survey 1983.

responded well to health educators and hence their health has improved, while social classes 4 and 5 still continue to eat inappropriate food and continue to smoke, so that now coronary heart disease is more common in these lower social classes. Other variations are less easy to explain and are part of the fascinating detective activity of the epidemiologist.

Within the health care system, social class may affect whether or not an individual consults his general practitioner (Table 14) and whether having done so he follows his advice or indeed whether he understands what the doctor says to

Table 10. Infant mortality 1975/76 – England and Wales (rates per 1000 live births).

Social class	Still births	Neonatal deaths (under 4 weeks)	Post neonatal deaths (1–11 months)
I + II	7.8	7.9	3.0
III	9.8	9.3	4.0
IV + V	12.0	11.7	6.1
Illegitimate	12.7	15.0	7.4

Source: Medical Statistics Division, OPCS, *Social and Biological Factors in Infant Mortality*, 1975–76, occasional paper No. 12 OPCS 1978.

Table 11. Health of school children, Scotland 1973. The figures record the percentage of school children at the age of five suffering from refractive error in eyesight and tooth decay. Average height is given for fourteen year olds.

Social class of parent	Refractive error in eyesight		Tooth decay		Height (cm)
	Boys	Girls	Boys	Girls	
I	3.7	2.9	6.7	8.2	157
II	3.6	5.4	8.3	9.4	156
III	4.6	4.6	14.5	15.7	155
IV	5.1	6.2	16.7	19.7	154
V	8.6	7.8	21.2	20.6	152.5
All classes	5.0	5.3	20.6	16.6	154

Source: Scottish Health Service.

him. Most medical staff are middle class in origin and do not know the words working-class people use to describe parts of their bodies and normal functions. Because of the

Table 12. Use of the school health services by children up to the age of seven, Great Britain 1965. The figures record the percentages of children who had never visited a dentist and who had never been immunized against smallpox, polio and diphtheria.

Social class of father	Dentist	Smallpox	Polio	Diphtheria
I	16	6	1	1
II	20	14	3	3
III non-manual	19	16	3	3
III manual	24	25	4	6
IV	27	29	6	8
V	31	33	10	11
All classes	23	23	5	6

Source: National Child Development Study.

Table 13. Persons reporting illness, rates per 1000, England and Wales 1976.

Socioeconomic grouping	Chronic sickness		Acute sickness restricted activity in a two-week period	
	Long-standing illness	Limiting long-standing		
	Males	Females	Males	Females	Males	Females
Professional	176	177	80	86	95	109
Employers	215	206	121	131	79	80
Intermediate and junior non-manual	245	266	147	163	92	106
Skilled manual	249	228	160	143	95	91
Semiskilled manual	276	312	178	213	78	104
Unskilled manual	345	432	234	299	100	103

Source: General Household Survey 1978.

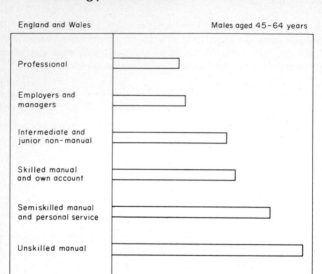

Figure 9. Males reporting limiting long-standing illness, 1972. *Source*: General Household Survey.

Table 14. Persons consulting a GP (NHS) in a 2-week reference period. Rates per 1000, England and Wales.

Socioeconomic groupings	Males	Females
Professional	69	120
Employers and managers	102	116
Intermediate and junior non-manual	104	127
Skilled manual	103	134
Semiskilled manual	112	143
Unskilled manual	138	157

Source: General Household Survey 1977.

feeling of inferiority many patients are unable or unwilling to ask questions or to indicate that they have not understood what has been said and therefore remain confused and in ignorance.

Sir Douglas Black, a past president of the Royal College of Physicians, describes these differences in the report of a working party entitled 'Inequalities of Care'.

The National Health Service is dominated by the medical profession and there is some evidence that much of it is run for their benefit rather than for the benefit of the patient. Emphasis is placed on 'scientific medicine', 'interesting cases' and 'good teaching material', to the detriment of the chronically sick, the elderly and the handicapped. Television programmes such as *Your Life in Their Hands* dramatically portray the power possessed by doctors. This power enables them to decide who is sick, who is well, what is health; and they dominate decisions relating to abortion, birth control and child health. One of the interesting developments in recent years has been the demand by many people to participate in their own treatment. This has been further demonstrated by many sick people turning to holistic medicine (often described as 'fringe' or 'alternative' medicine) as this enables them to take part in setting goals for their own treatment and care and emphasizes the importance of the total person rather than just concentrating on the disease.

SOCIAL MOBILITY

Classes, as we have seen, tend to develop a self-consciousness and solidarity and this is enhanced by the degree with which they are self-recruiting. This may be almost 100% if societies restrict the individual's opportunity to 'better himself' or to change his occupation. However, in most industrial societies, because of reasonable access to education and/or jobs, it is widely believed that a person's social class is achieved rather than ascribed and that social mobility opportunities are substantial, despite the difficulties.

To measure social mobility, sociologists compare the status of the father with that of his son (occupation is used as the index of status); this is intergenerational mobility. Change within a generation, intragenerational mobility, is assessed by looking at the occupational grouping in which a man starts his working life and that within which he ends his working days. There are problems in both these measurements. In the first it is not known when the sons studied have reached the height of their career. In recent years there has been a change in occupational structure, for example a decline in agriculture and an increase in technical work and non-manual occupations; there has also been a change in the relative fertility rates of different classes and therefore recruitment into non-manual occupations may occur from families where the previous pattern was one of manual work.

A study carried out by the London School of Economics found that in each of the Registrar General's groups less than half the sons were the same status as their fathers; one-fifth of the highest group fathers had sons who were downwardly mobile by two to three categories and the same number of the lowest group fathers had sons who were upwardly mobile by two to three categories.

Movement within a generation is more restricted and, with education becoming a determining factor of occupation, it could decrease further, unless the trend towards retraining of adults increases in which case an individual may have more than one occupational career in life. In this case change and hence mobility will increase. High unemployment levels may result in people taking jobs below their educational achievement expectations; in this case downward mobility occurs.

Social mobility may be determined by the occupational structure of the society, by cultural factors such as access to education, differential fertility rates and individual motivation. The latter aspect is affected by the norms of society and the family and class of origin. Evidence shows that upwardly mobile children are likely to have been encouraged by their parents to become independent and to have been socialized into an expectation of higher grouping. Such famiies, in fact, may well have adopted the norms and life-style of the class above their own. In recent years many of these families have rejected the State comprehensive school and have paid for their children to attend independent schools.

The access to knowledge relating to occupations is also affected by family of origin. The working-class child is less likely to know anything about a career in law, accountancy or medicine and is more likely to follow the career of an admired relative, father, brother or uncle, than to branch out into something new. As in education, his peer group will also influence his choice and a desire for a safe job or 'good money now' may result in him being an 'under-achiever' in terms of career.

EMBOURGEOISEMENT

Despite the arguments for class solidarity and the stereotyped images of the white-collar or the cloth cap, there is a claim made that class lines are blurring and that the distinctions between manual and non-manual workers are disappearing. The argument is based on the fact that income levels are less clearly defined and that the increase in the money earned by many of the working class has led to their adopting a middle-class life-style. However, adoption of a way of life in terms of possessions does not mean that they have also adopted the same attitudes. A study of car workers suggests that *embourgeoisement* may occur in three stages. In the first or 'privatized' stage the worker's interest becomes home centred and there is a decline in his involvement with the traditional working-class community and its norms. In the second stage he begins to aspire to become a member of the middle class, accepting their way of life and hoping that they will accept him. Only when this assimilation of the worker into the middle class has taken place can the third stage of embourgeoisement be said to have occurred.

The situation is therefore that there are a number of the working class who have rejected the status of their class but as yet have not achieved middle-class status. This is likely to affect their pattern of expenditure and may result in a change in attitudes affecting such things as voting behaviour or education provided for their children but does not necessarily indicate that the social classes are merging.

The perpetuation of social inequalities is argued by some to be essential for society. It has been stated that social status is a device '. . . by which societies ensure that the most important positions are filled by the most qualified persons. Hence every society, no matter how simple or complex, must differentiate persons in terms of both prestige and esteem, and must therefore possess a certain amount of institutionalized inequality' (Davies and Moore, 1945). This statement, however, fails to note the disfunctional effects of stratification and also does not differentiate between merit and class, but is primarily an argument for the necessity of unequal rewards for positions of unequal importance. This produces an argument that tends to become circular: that the most important positions are most highly rewarded because they are the most important! This argument also assumes no barriers to the development of talents and pays little account to the inequality of access to recruitment training and even motivation. Class systems may therefore limit the supply of talent. Others in society continue to maintain their position because it is to their advantage and not necessarily to the advantage of the community.

References and Further Reading

Bendix, R. & Lipset, S.M. (1953) *Class Status and Power*. London: Routledge & Kegan Paul.

Bernstein, B. (1958) Some sociological determinants of perception. *British Journal of Sociology*, **9**.

Bernstein, B. (1971) *Class Codes and Control*, Vol. 1. London: Routledge & Kegan Paul.

Black, D. (1980) *Inequalities in Health: Report of a Working Group*. London: DHSS.

Burns, T. (ed.) (1969) *Industrial Man*, Sections 1 and 2. Harmondsworth: Penguin.

Butterworth, E. & Weir, D. (1974) *The Sociology of Modern Britain*, Sections 4 and 5. London: Fontana.

Central Advisory Council for Education (1967) *Plowden Report. Children and their Primary Schools*. London: HMSO.

Chief Medical Officer of Health's Report, published annually. London: HMSO.

Committee on Nursing (1972) *Briggs Report. Report of the Committee on Nursing*. London: HMSO.

Davies, K. & Moore, W.E. (1945) Some principles of stratification. *American Sociological Review*, **10**, 2.

Glass D.V. (ed.) (1954) *Social Mobility in Britain*. London: Routledge & Kegan Paul.

Goffman, E. (1968) *Stigma*. London: Pelican.

Goldthorpe, J.H. & Lockwood, D. (1970) The changing national class structure. In Butterworth, E. & Weir, D. (eds) *The Sociology of Modern Britain*. London: Fontana.

McIntosh, M.E. & Woodley, A. (1974) The Open University and second chance education. *Paedagogica Europaea*, **9**, 85–100.

Ministry of Education (1963) *Robbins Report. Higher Education: A Report of the Committee on Higher Education*. London: HMSO.

Office of Population Censuses and Surveys. *General Household Survey, 1976, 1977, 1978, 1983*. London: HMSO.

Reid, I. (1977) *Social Class Differences in Britain: A Source Book*. London: Open Books.

Scotson, J. (1975) *Introducing Society*, Chapters 4 and 5. London: Routledge & Kegan Paul.

Social Trends. London: Central Statistical Office, published annually.

Thompson, E.P. (1963) *The Making of the English Working Class*. Harmondsworth: Penguin.

Tuckett, D. (1976) *An Introduction to Medical Sociology*, Chapter 4. London: Tavistock.

Turner, R.H. (1964) Sponsored and contest mobility and the school system. *American Sociological Review*, **25**.

Weber, M. (1920) *The Theory of Social and Economic Organisations* translated by Parsons, T. (1964). New York: Free Press.

Worsley, P. (ed.) (1977) *Modern Sociology, Introductory Readings*, Parts 5, 6 and 8. Harmondsworth: Penguin.

7 Gender in Society and Health Care

One of the more obvious and yet controversial forms of stratification in society is that of gender. At one time, the latter part of the previous sentence would not have been true, as it was taken for granted that not only were there physiological differences between men and women, but that these differences applied throughout *all* areas of life with, in almost all cases, the woman being seen as the weaker and inferior sex. To a certain extent, this situation still applies, despite efforts to change it by women from the time of the suffragettes through to today's feminist movements.

In the chapter on socialization, we have considered the way boys and girls are taught to play the male or female role, starting with the colour of their baby clothes, via toys, to the jobs they are expected to have, whether allowed to exhibit sensitivity, or cry when hurt. It is true that many countries are making efforts to change the pattern of socialization, showing pictures in books of boys playing with dolls and girls with aeroplanes; nevertheless, the stereotype exists, little girls being made of 'sugar and spice and all things nice', while it's 'frogs and snails and puppy dogs' tails, that's what little boys are made of'.

One of the greatest areas of social change in Western society in recent years has been in the position of women. Their fight for equal opportunity with men has been long and often acrimonious, despite their contribution in two world wars. One area in which this change has progressed is with regard to the legal rights of women in marriage and divorce. The married woman is now legally recognized as an independent individual and does not have to have her husband's permission to enter into contracts, although some hire purchase firms still ask for a male sponsor! She has equality in divorce, division of property and rights over children.

Figures relating to marriage breakdown are always difficult to analyse because of the changes that have occurred in law over the past 130 years. In 1857, divorce required an Act of Parliament and cost about £700, so naturally it was reserved for the rich. Also, divorce was restricted to proof of adultery by the wife, the woman having no access to divorce herself. During the beginning of this century, various Acts were passed altering the grounds for divorce, and eventually, in 1923, allowing the wife to sue for divorce on the grounds of adultery by her husband. The cost still remained high and therefore separation remained the commonest solution to a broken marriage. However, in 1947 it became possible to claim financial assistance as 'Legal Aid'. Since the Divorce Reform Act, 1969, divorce has been possible on the grounds that the marriage has broken down and that, by mutual consent, the partners wish it dissolved; the question of innocent or guilty partners does not apply.

These factors may help to account for the increases in divorce rates as shown in Figure 10.

There are now few restricted fields in employment (one is the Anglican clergy) and the Sex Discrimination Act protects women against discrimination in the matter of equal pay for equal work. However, inequalities still remain. Fewer women achieve higher education and many employers still prefer to employ men, feeling that women are less reliable, putting their families before their jobs. Certainly, there remains a conflict between the role of mother and the pursuit of a career, despite legislation relating to maternity leave.

The number of women in the professions has increased, but still remains low in proportion to the total number employed. Apart from teaching, nursing and social work, women are under-represented at the top of any professional group and, even in these conventionally 'women's professions', men are rapidly taking over the top posts. Indeed, for women to get to the top in any of the professions they

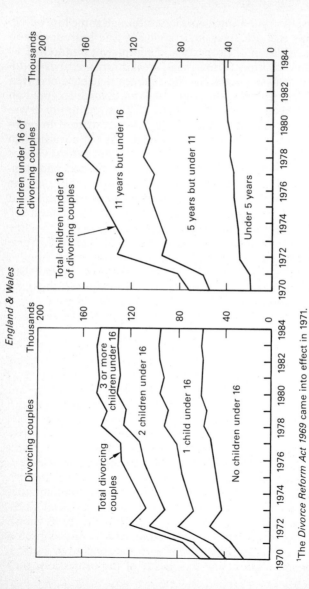

England & Wales

Divorcing couples

Children under 16 of divorcing couples

Total divorcing couples

3 or more children under 16
2 children under 16
1 child under 16
No children under 16

Total children under 16 of divorcing couples

11 years but under 16
5 years but under 11
Under 5 years

[1] The *Divorce Reform Act 1969* came into effect in 1971.

Figure 10. Divorcing couples: by number and age of children. *Source*: Office of Population Censuses and Surveys.

frequently have to be 'better' than the men to get any degree of 'equality' in respect and consideration for the post.

Although the 1975 Sex Discrimination Act was passed to provide equality of opportunity for women, they are still under-represented in Parliament, the Cabinet (despite a woman Prime Minister), in law, in universities above the lecturer grade, and so on.

Outside the professions, women tend to have low aspirations, thinking of the job more in terms of money than as a career, and the fact that women are traditionally poorly unionized has helped to perpetuate the low wages paid to them in many industries.

The effect on the country of the change in their position has been far reaching. The two-wage family has resulted in higher standards of living and greater spending capacity. Coupled with this has been an increased demand for social services such as crèches, play-groups, day nurseries and home helps to care for the sick or aged. Increased unemployment in the 1980s has also increased the previously unusual situation of the woman being the wage earner while the man has cared for the house and children.

Figure 11 demonstrates that this increase in female economic activity is not restricted to the United Kingdom, although it is high in comparison to many countries.

NURSE–DOCTOR RELATIONSHIP

The nurse–doctor relationship is a complex one, affected to a great degree by the fact that doctors are most frequently male and nurses female, hence male dominance and female subjection. One of the areas of conflict within the relationship is the inconsistency of the doctor, who requires the nurse to be his 'handmaiden' while he is present, but expects her to assume responsibility for complex treatments and recognition of diagnostic signs in his absence. The historical reasons for this situation are clear. Medicine is well recognized as a profession, while nursing is still developing and

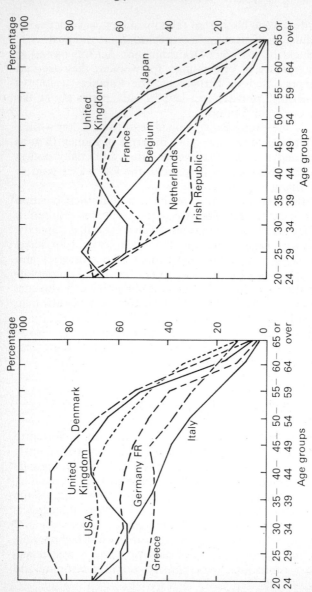

Figure 11. Female economic activity rates: by age, international comparison, 1983. *Source:* Labour Force Survey 1983, Department of Employment; Japanese Labour Force Survey; Employment and Earnings, US Bureau of Labor Statistics.

may not have clear-cut professional characteristics. Secondly, society, while it frequently gives high status to nurses (A 1970s survey placed them top of the list in public esteem), nevertheless gives greater monetary rewards to medical practitioners.

Another attitude held by some doctors towards the nurses with whom they work is that of paternalism. Although expressing gratitude for services rendered, either to the patient on their behalf or to themselves, there is always a degree of surprise that the nurse was capable of such a high standard of care. Such doctors frequently talk about 'my' nurses and, while treating them kindly, do not take much account of any views they may hold. In fairness to the doctors, they are often adored by their nurses, who will do anything for them; whether this is a case of self-selection or socialization, it is hard to say.

Obviously, these views will affect the nurse's perception of herself and then her perception of her interaction with the patient. The nurse who feels markedly subordinate to the doctor is more likely to carry out tasks allocated to her and obey instructions, but less likely to use her initiative, or to perceive other than the clinical needs of the patient. The 'wonderful nurse' who can see no wrong in the doctor will also be conscientious in obeying orders, intensely loyal and unlikely to question routine, even though she may realize that there may be other methods of practice. Only where the nurse can see herself as a colleague, with the right to express an opinion, will she look at each situation with critical eyes and realize that no two patients are alike and hence the need for flexibility in the provision of care.

Of course, there is the doctor who treats the nurse as a colleague, respecting her opinions on the care of the patient, appreciating that her constant contact is likely to provide a much clearer insight into the patient's condition than his more transitory medical examination.

The presence in the nursing profession of an increasing number of male nurses and the voice given to nurses at organizational level are beginning to affect the nurse–doctor relationships. Some doctors certainly resent the fact that nurses wish to control their own affairs and feel that promotion into administrative levels of 'their' ward sisters has resulted in a lowering of the standard of patient care. Unfortunately, the effects of rapid patient movement, early discharge, shorter working hours and the increase in number of untrained staff (auxiliaries and learners) in proportion to trained staff are rarely considered.

In recent years, courses have been developed which provide the nurse with higher education leading to a degree, either in nursing or in another discipline associated with nursing, such as sociology or human biology. Graduates of these courses have also met with opposition from many members of the medical profession. There is widespread suspicion of the 'academic' nurse. While the clever doctor or lawyer is spoken of with awe, the clever nurse is usually subjected to the accusation that she is no good 'practically'. The logic of this is difficult to understand and it is not backed up by research, though the idea is not restricted to nursing: indeed, in all occupations which have a manual component, there is resistance to the 'thinker'.

Miss Nightingale had a clear view of the role of the nurse. In 1867, writing to one of her students who had become a matron, she said: 'The whole reform in nursing, both at home and abroad, has consisted in this: to take all power out of the hands of the men and put it into the hands of one female trained head and make her responsible for everything (regarding internal management and discipline) being carried out . . . Do not let the doctor make himself Head Nurse!' This is as appropriate now, over 100 years later, as then.

The Male Nurse

If the female nurse feels discriminated against because of her sex, rewarded with poor pay and patronized by doctors and politicians, then it is true that most men in nursing, other than in the psychiatric field, have also at some time suffered discrimination, as shown by the fact that we actually talk about a 'male' nurse as if a freak. The traditional view of the man as the hunter and fighter does not easily allow other virtues of compassion and tenderness to be displayed. Yet these are the virtues commonly attributed to the nurse and indeed make nursing the unique activity that it is. Of course, nursing needs not only those with so-called feminine traits, caring, empathy and compassion, but it also needs those with the so-called masculine traits of technical and scientific decision-making.

No man is entirely masculine in personality and no woman entirely feminine, and it is the balance of these traits that makes the individual unique. Both are needed in the provision of nursing care and the contribution made by the nurse who is male will be as complex in balance as that given by the nurse who is female. The fact that men are over-represented in managerial posts in nursing may be due to this difference in balance of traits, or it may be due to the conventional male/female stereotyping, which assumes that men are 'better' in managerial posts and 'need' the better salaries that accompany such posts as they are the family breadwinner. It does appear to be true that the drive for better pay for all nurses has been given a major impetus by the men in nursing.

The Token Person

One result of the raising of society's consciousness regarding the discrimination that may occur, based on gender as well as on race and colour, has been the emergence of the 'token' man or woman. This person is invited to serve on committees, or is given employment where the other gender is overwhelmingly predominant, so that it can be said that the group does not discriminate. The position of this token individual is then manipulated in such a way that his or her contribution is stifled. Experience of this in the past as a token female nurse in a predominantly medical and male setting resulted in any suggestions that consideration should be given to normative aspects of care, or that findings other than those of a double-blind clinical trial were worthy of consideration, being dismissed as emotional and illogical.

The presence of men in nursing, although still in a minority, and the constantly increasing number of women in medicine, may well alter the whole pattern of interaction within the health care setting. Obviously, what is needed is not that one gender or profession should be seen as superior and the other inferior, but that both recognize their complementary contribution. Tschudin (1985) comments, 'By copying men, nurses do not become equals with them but rather degrade their femininity. By copying women, men do not become better nurses but degrade their own maleness.'

Health Care of Women

The fact that most doctors are male has an impact on the way women receive health care. Part of this is due to the ambivalent approach to female physiology. While menstruation, childbirth and the menopause are 'natural' and therefore no fuss should be made of them, paradoxically they are also considered to be a threat to a woman's physical and mental stability. For many years, menstrual tension, pain, post-partum depression and menopausal symptoms were seen as evidence of a woman's 'erratic' behaviour. There has been limited research into these conditions and many are treated symptomatically, rather than by seeking the cause.

In the same way, women are frequently given tranquillizers and/or antidepressants by doctors who fail to realize that the physical symptoms may be the result of social pressures and frustration.

Any woman who deviates from the traditional female role finds herself under considerable social pressure. Smart (1976) comments that many women find the traditional role unacceptable and that it is this that produces a high incidence of mental illness in women. Brown and Harris (1978) also found that the incidence of depression in women in East London was closely correlated with their social situation.

Webb (1985) found negative attitudes to ill women were not confined to doctors, but were also demonstrated by some female nurses, particularly when the patient had a gynaecological condition.

The problem is that the woman is frequently seen as a deviant. The career woman is a deviant, but so it must be said is the unemployed man. A working mother is a severe deviant and, as Lorber (1975) has said, 'Female patients are compounded deviants — they are defined as ill by virtue of their reproductive functions; they are also held responsible for whatever is disabling, difficult to manage, or disruptive about these functions; and finally, they are devalued for reacting emotionally to their physical condition.'

The male/female stereotype is often a problem to the nurse when confronted with a patient in pain. Men are expected to be tough and uncomplaining so their pain is often not appreciated and, if a man does demonstrate distress, he may be labelled a 'sissy'. On the other hand, women's pain is often under-appreciated because they are considered to be making a fuss.

As can be seen from this chapter, and indeed all others, where individuals are labelled and classified, such categorization removes from that person his or her unique individuality and frequently results in lack of appropriate care. Nurses are constantly reminded that care should be 'individualized'; society, by its labels and stereotypes, demonstrates the opposite view. Nurses, as members of society, must be on their guard.

References and Further Reading

Austin, R. (1977) Sex and gender in the future of nursing. Nos. 1 & 2. *Nursing Times*, August 25, September 1.

Brown, G. & Harris, T. (1978) *Social Origins of Depression*. London: Tavistock.

Brown, R. & Stones, R. (1973) *The Male Nurse*. Occasional paper. Society of Administration Research Trust.

Delamont, S. (1980) *The Sociology of Women: An Introduction*. London: Allen & Unwin.

Gavon, H. (1966) *The Captive Wife*. Harmondsworth: Penguin.

Lorber, J. (1975) Women and medical sociology. In Millman, M. and Kaster, R.M. (eds) *Another Voice*. New York: Anchor Books.

Smart, C. (1976) *Women, Crime and Criminology*. London: Routledge & Kegan Paul.

Snavely, B.K. & Fairhurst, G.T. (1984) The male nursing student as a token. *Research in Nursing & Health*, 7, 287–294.

Townsend, P. (1973) *The Social Minority*. London: Allen Lane.

Tschudin, V. (1985) *Nursing—A Balanced Profession*. Prize-winning Essay, The Baillière Prize for Nursing Studies.

Webb, C. (1985) Gynaecological nursing: a compromising situation. *Journal of Advanced Nursing*, **10**, 47–54.

8 Nursing as an Occupation

Despite many definitions, most people would agree that nursing is essentially a social activity, an interaction process between two individuals, the nurse and the patient. Even when a group of patients is cared for by a team of nurses the actual task is one where individuals react with individuals. The unit then is two people and what happens when they meet, and it is interesting to note that Timasheff (1966) uses virtually the same definition when introducing the study of sociology. If sociology and nursing share a similar definition, it is likely that the study of the one may provide insights for the study of the other and that sociological theories may contribute to the development of theory in nursing.

Professor J.K. McFarlane (1970) states: 'The unique function of the nurse is to give nursing care. To this function both nursing management and nursing education are in a service relationship. Their excellence can only be judged by the excellence of nursing care which they enable.' The definition and this statement appear to emphasize task performance in nursing and indeed this is how many people, including nurses, view it. Various studies have shown the value placed on 'getting through the work' and on colleagues who 'pull their weight' (Altschul, 1972; Anderson, 1973).

This task orientation is further supported by the way in which work in hospital wards is organized. A study carried out for the Committee on Nursing (1972), the Briggs Report, showed that despite lip service paid to concepts such as *total patient care* or *team nursing* 61% of nurses in general hospitals were allocated work on a 'task' basis (*task allocation*). Tasks varied from domestic to highly skilled but because of the 'production line' approach there was a tendency for the patient to be reduced to a series of functions instead of being seen as an individual and the centre of the activity. The Briggs Report comments on this, stating: 'We are convinced that the right approach is a patient-orientated one, but in stating our conviction we wish to add that this approach can be achieved by means of a variety of systems. However work is organized, it can be analysed in terms of tasks to be performed, the important thing is to keep the focus on the patient at all times as the centre and origin of all the activities undertaken.' In recent years nursing has adopted a more rational and scientific approach to nursing care. This involves the taking of a nursing history in which relevant information relating to the patient as a psycho-social as well as a biological individual is collected. From these data an assessment of patient needs is made and a plan of nursing care is drawn up in which the nurse and the patient agree on the goals to be achieved (both in the short and long term) and steps are taken either to enable the patient to meet his own needs or for the nurse to assist or meet them for him.

Finally, evaluation is carried out on a continuing basis and the nursing plan adjusted as required. This sequence of action is usually called the 'nursing process'; certainly it is a process in which nursing focuses on the patient as an individual rather than on a medical diagnosis or on a list of tasks to be performed.

In addition, nursing theories and models have been developed which help focus attention on the aim of nursing intervention. For example, the model may be one of 'meeting the patient's needs' (Henderson, 1962), assisting with 'activities of living' (Roper, 1976), identifying methods by which 'adaptation' to illness may be assisted (Roy, 1974), or studying the way in which nurse–patient activity achieves goals (King, 1971).

Nursing has often been the subject of sociological study and it has been explained that part of its fascination for the sociologist is that it often appears to be the occupation that is the 'exception that proves the rule'. One of these exceptions exists in the theory propounded by Parsons (1964) that within organizations there exists a tendency to separate instrumental or task-orientated functions from those that are expressive, that is, demand an emotional content. The assumption is that to attain organizational goals and to maintain role clarity these functions cannot be fulfilled by the same person in the same work place at the same time. However, the ideology of the nursing profession, and indeed the tasks performed, demand that the nurse operates in both these areas simultaneously. In fact, the situation is even more complicated in that for patients as a whole, as met in a ward or department, the nurse is expected to treat everyone alike, in Parsonian terms to show *universalism* and 'affective neutrality', but when dealing with the individual patients within the same setting she is both taught and expected to show individual concern, *particularism*, and to demonstrate empathy or *affectivity*. It is obvious then that the role of the nurse is likely to arouse conflict both within herself and in her relationship with others.

MOTIVATION TO NURSE

When a nurse is asked why she commenced nursing as a career the first answer usually given is interest in people and the desire to care for or help them. This type of answer is often considered to reinforce the idea of nursing as a vocation, indicating if not a call from God, at least an overwhelming urge to give oneself to the care of others. Motivation of this type does not emphasize return to health for the patient but concentrates on what is normally an intermediate goal for the patient, that of care.

As an alternative to the physical care motivation of the nurse, others may be driven by a different need, that of knowledge. A few nurses, if honest, will admit that they really wanted to study medicine or one of the biological sciences and that their main interest is in the academic and/or technical aspects of nursing. This is not to say that such people cannot also give excellent physical care while being fascinated by the developments of medical science but it may account for the ease with which some nurses adopt the medical model of nursing and regard the patient as a case or a disease. An extension of this situation may be excessive attention to machines or equipment, resulting in complaints by the patient about physical care being overlooked, thus indicating that the maintenance of the machine or the performance of a technique has become a goal.

It is probable that nurses thus motivated will be ready and anxious to accept from the doctor tasks which are not traditionally regarded as nursing care. This has already happened in that procedures such as reading the blood pressure or taking blood samples are now commonly regarded as nursing tasks and there is a likelihood that others will follow. Although many nursing leaders in the United States and the United Kingdom see this as undesirable in that it implies a dependence on the medical profession rather than an area of competence specific to the nurse, in other countries it is welcomed. Sweden attributes the recruitment of highly intelligent girls and low wastage to the fact that Swedish nurses give anaesthetics and set up intravenous infusions, and therefore have higher prestige than nurses in some other countries due to their close relationship with medical skills.

In the United Kingdom medically orientated nurses, when trained, probably seek work in areas such as intensive care and renal dialysis where equipment is likely to be intricate and of vital importance, rather than in those areas requiring mainly basic physical care of the patient, such as geriatric nursing, or long-stay medical wards for the chronically sick. This does not necessarily mean that patients in these units do not receive adequate physical care but inevitably there is a danger that they may be made to feel merely an appendage to a machine.

Nurses may prefer work in these areas to satisfy yet another personal goal, that of social mobility. In these areas the nurses work closely with the doctor as a member of the team and therefore tend to feel that their position is more prestigious. The use of nursing as a conscious avenue of social mobility is clearly seen in some developing countries where nurses enjoy high status and this may also apply to immigrants in the United Kingdom. However, where physical care is regarded as degrading, the intimate requirements of a patient may be either ignored or dealt with in a perfunctory manner. (It is possible for nursing as a profession to have high status even though physical care is considered degrading: often perceptions of status relate to the top of the hierarchy and the practical work and intermediate steps are ignored.) In spite of teaching the new entrant to the profession that all patients are served without reference to race, creed or class, cultural or individual bias may result in the favouring of some patients because of their status. Again, some nurses with a primary motivation towards social mobility may provide excellent physical care and regard all patients as equal while in contact with them but it is unlikely that their career will be one that involves remaining at the bedside. It is unfortunate, in a society which equates money with status, that nurses who carry out patient care are poorly paid. Indeed this tends to be true in all occupations, more money and therefore greater status is awarded to those who occupy managerial positions. Only where the practitioner is fully autonomous is this situation not apparent — this, according to some, is the hallmark of a true professional.

The pattern of motivation shown by a nurse and the type of care provided may be seen as a demonstration of '*social exchange*'.

WHAT NURSES DO

There have been many studies observing the nurse in the ward and these have all revealed a wide range of tasks covered in a normal day, ranging from giving the patient physical care, talking to the patient, keeping records, answering the telephone, doing the flowers, accompanying doctors on rounds and so on. All these may have a direct or indirect impact on patient care but what is enlightening is the relative importance of these tasks in the eyes of the nurse and in the eyes of the patient. Patients frequently express a desire for more personal contact with the nurse whereas nurses obviously demonstrate a greater 'task' than patient orientation. This 'task-centred' activity is usually decried when nurses are questioned but is said to be inevitable due to organizational structure and/or shortage of staff. However, relieving nurses of non-nursing duties or an increase in numbers of staff available on a ward at any one time tends to show only a very slight increase in the time spent with the patients; instead the extra time is spent in administrative duties or in nurses chatting together.

Reasons for this are not clear. Isabel Menzies (1960) sees it as a defence against anxiety produced by close contact with patients. Certainly nurses do find constant contact with the ill stressful and in the past used cleaning or going on errands to departments as a relief from the ward situation. If this is so then it is possible that removal of these outlets due to the implementation of the Salmon Report (Committee on Senior Nursing Staff Structures, 1966) may have resulted in higher sickness, absenteeism and wastage. Alternatively the trained nurse may increasingly seek areas of work, such as administration, which remove her from close contact with the patient. This 'flight from the bedside' is condemned by the nursing profession as a body and by most commentators, either medical or lay, of the nursing scene. Many nurses who have taken posts away from the bedside are made to feel guilty and assert that the reason is money or lack of prestige. Letters received by the Committee on Nursing implied that the attitudes and behaviour to nurses was such that 'there seems to be complete disregard for the human being beneath the nurse' and that 'training tends to destroy initiative, discretion, common sense and dampens the enthusiasm which most nurses have to get, to know and look after ill people.' This condemnation of the way in which the neophyte is treated on entering the nursing profession is a serious reflection both on the education and training offered and also the organization as the context in which it takes place. It has been suggested that three factors have modified the original character of the nurse's role:

1. the degree of standardization of tasks and procedures demanded by the administrative hierarchy;
2. the limited degree of authority permitted in the clinical situation; and
3. the peculiar relationship of the nurse to organizational means and goals which may be expressed in terms of efficiency and standards.

One of the results of the nurse being employed in patient care in the hospital rather than the home environment is the emphasis that is placed on routine organizational requirements such as record keeping and working within boundaries set to preserve the safety and the stability of the organization.

The primary goal of the hospital could be considered as diagnosis and treatment leading to cure, although in teaching hospitals emphasis may be placed on teaching and research (the latter may or may not include the prevention of disease). However, hospitals have increased in size and specialization within them has also increased which has resulted in increasing bureaucratization. Increases in complexity and specialization produce great emphasis on the importance of records. All the people concerned with treatment and care of any individual patient are no longer able to meet in a face-to-face relationship and therefore a formalized system of communication becomes essential. Not only that, but memories can no longer cope with the mass of information available relating to any individual patient and therefore the importance of record keeping has developed. To ensure rapid and accurate retrieval of these data patients need to be given numbers and this may increase a feeling of loss of individuality. The use of individual patient 'nursing' records as in the nursing process may help counteract this, as may the development of the 'primary nurse'. This is a nurse who has the prime responsibility for planning the care of the patient and accepts accountability for the end-result of this care.

A formal administrative structure is also needed to service the activities of the professionals within the organization, such persons having clearly defined areas of responsibility and a hierarchical role structure. It has been argued that one of the definitions of professionalism is that of the ratio of 'indetermination/technicality' within an occupation, professionals scoring high in indeterminacy and administrators in technicality. To ensure that records are efficiently kept, budgeting and expenditure controlled, communications established and order maintained, rules are formulated relating to the way everyday activities are carried out and so paper work proliferates. It is customary for all not actively engaged in administration to regard this paper work as administrative red tape which gets in the way of the 'real' work and yet if the system breaks down these same people are the first to complain. Bureaucracy at its best can provide order, continuity and a certain degree of predictability in an organization concerned with many and diverse activities.

However, in a manner common to most organizations, a large amount of a hospital's resources have to be devoted to self-maintenance. Such organizational goal displacement may make it virtually impossible for employees to maintain their personal primary goals and as in the case of the nurse they may find that their role is defined in almost exclusively supervisory and administrative terms rather than related to therapy or care, and the definition of a 'good' nurse may be related to her knowledge of the rules of the organization and to her ability to enforce them. Nurses are frequently rewarded, through increased status, mainly for skills not including direct patient contact, for example, keeping records, operating technical equipment, teaching and supervising.

Part of this goal displacement is related to the desire of the nurse for prestige and status. At one time this was achieved due to the nurse's close contact with the doctor who was seen as a prestigious person. With the attempt by nurses to achieve an independent professional status her place as coordinator and leader of the health team in the ward situation is stressed and in many cases direct patient care is delegated to others, for example nursing auxiliaries. There is, therefore, an area of conflict, a professional ethos which emphasizes the importance of the nurse–patient relationship and an ideological commitment to the ideal of bedside care (note the efforts that nurses who work away from the bedside either as teachers or administrators make to justify their work in terms of ultimate benefit to the patients) and an organizational structure that demands an increase in supervisory and administrative functions.

Individual goals may also remain unfulfilled, especially if they are strictly vocational in character. Modern organizations have little place for the individual whose activities are a result of guidance by God and who may wish to devote more time to individual patients than the demands of the ward allow. The advent of 'general managers' following the implementation of the Griffiths Report re-emphasizes the possible conflict between efficient cost-effective management and an individualized approach to care.

Professional authority is based on what the professional believes is right and therefore doctors and nurses demand freedom to act on the basis of professional skill and judgement on behalf of the individual patient. Any decision as to the rightness of the specific action may be made from outside the bureaucratic structure by fellow professionals, for example nurses obtain their licence to practice from outside the organization, that is from the UK Central Council (UKCC) for Nursing, Midwifery and Health Visiting, which also exercises a disciplinary function. Nevertheless, as already discussed, adherence to the organization's rules makes for a dependability and predictability. Fortunately these two legitimate claims on the way nurses should behave do not often clash but when they do they may profoundly affect the nurse–patient or nurse–doctor relationships. The UKCC's Code of Professional Conduct makes it clear that the nurse's prime responsibility is to the patient. Nevertheless, several cases in recent years have demonstrated the power of the organization over professional judgement. The individual's position in the organizational structure plays a part in shaping his perspective to the rules. The houseman (junior hospital doctor) by definition is only in the area temporarily and for comparatively short periods of time, his main goal being learning. The ward sister, however, is there all the time and has to maintain the normal routine for the patients over the whole day and also provide a sense of continuity. The smooth running of the unit is appreciated by the doctor while he is there but he is frequently unaware of how it is achieved. The real problem arises when the nurse is unable to suspend the rules to deal with emergency occurrences and unable to tolerate change. Unfortunately it is relatively easy for rule-keeping to be observed and therefore rewards may be given for good records, clean and tidy wards, rather than for the less easily assessed task of meeting the patient's goals and needs. In fact goal displacement frequently occurs and there is a tendency to develop a 'trained incapacity' to deal with change. An excellent example of this was observed in an employment agency (Blau, 1969), when it was announced that a record would be kept of the number of clients seen. The number of interviews rose but there was less attempt made to fit the job to the client which was the primary goal of the organization. A similar danger exists in hospitals due to the emphasis placed on bed occupancy and turnover rates. Some observers feel that the goal of many hospital staff is the discharge of the patient whether dead or alive instead of treatment and care resulting in a change of their previous state.

In nursing a similar displacement of goals may occur, hence the stories, which unfortunately are not apocryphal, of the patient being wakened out of a deep sleep to take sleeping pills. Patients are individuals and as such do not conform to closely laid down standards and rules. Nursing, therefore, needs to be guided by basic principles so that individual variation can be tolerated and rules kept to the minimum. This allows for the action required in emergency situations which might otherwise be labelled as deviant and ensures that rewards are not given for conformity but for achievement of professionally acceptable goals. The reason for certain nursing tasks may not be immediately obvious. They can be described in terms of 'function'. The *manifest function* being the reason given for its performance, but the *latent function*, often poorly recognized, might be more important (Merton, 1957). An example of this can be seen in the changes brought about by early ambulation of patients: as recently as thirty-five years ago patients were kept in bed following surgery until the stitches were removed (approximately ten days) and frequently they were not allowed to wash themselves. During this time, therefore, they required a high level of personal care and this gave the nurse ample opportunity to talk to the patient while engaged in a physical task. The manifest function of a bed bath was to achieve the patient's personal cleanliness. However, the pseudo-privacy provided by the screens and the undivided attention of the nurse supported a latent function whereby the nurse had the opportunity to get to know the patient as an individual and the patient could discuss his fears and anxieties in a way that would not have been possible in a casual encounter. However, further developments in medical science subsequently suggested that wounds properly sutured do not give way during normal activity, and the pulmonary embolus that many patients developed and from which some died could often be traced to this long period of immobility. Therefore the pattern has now changed and it is rare for patients to be kept completely in bed even after major surgery. A serious problem has arisen from this change in practice, since patients require less physical care of a type that allows nurses easy opportunity to talk to the patient other than to issue instructions. The fact that the average length of stay in hospital for the patient with an acute illness has also decreased has further reduced the opportunity for the nurse and the patient to form a relationship which facilitates meaningful conversation. In view of this it might be argued that in the wards which house long-stay or chronic sick patients this situation would not occur. However, there is likely to be a shortage of staff on these wards and therefore the pressure is 'to get things done', so once again less time will be spent talking to the patient. Thus in most situations the traditional emphasis on activity, that is the fulfilling of the manifest function, still produces feelings of guilt in the nurse who is 'only' talking to the patient and hence the psychosocial needs of the patient are often disregarded and he is left with the feeling that nobody cares. It is an interesting comment on the nurse's perception of her role that although she has been relieved of many non-nursing duties by the employment of ward clerks and housekeeping teams, little, if any, of the time saved is spent in contact with the patients.

NURSE—PATIENT INTERACTION

The goal of the patient may in fact not be that of either the nurse or the organization. Usually it is return to health but, because this goal may be remote in time, patients often see it as the final of several intermediate goals such as freedom from pain, removal of an offending organ, ability to get out of bed, discharge from hospital and return to work. Obviously this is not a totally inclusive list nor is the order fixed, and many patients realize that they may have to accept one of the intermediate goals as a substitute for the final one in that return to health is apparently impossible. Progress in medical science frequently pushes back subsidiary goals so that more may be achieved and goals previously out of reach become realistic aims. Maslow (1943) proposed a theory of sequential development of goals relating to all individuals, dividing 'needs' or 'wants' into lower and higher categories, arguing that a lower want must be satisfied before the individual proceeds to the next and when this has been satisfied a yet 'higher' want emerges. He specified these goals or needs in the following terms:

1. physiological needs
2. safety needs

3. belongingness and love needs
4. esteem needs, for self and others
5. need for self-actualization

This ladder appears to fit quite well with the normal 'history' of the patient. However, this is not a rigid hierarchy and there are times when a specific need will assume prominence over all others, for example relief from pain which is acute, will at that moment be the paramount need; esteem needs may be felt strongly during some moments of indignity experienced during medical or nursing techniques.

Nonetheless the picture of a type of 'pilgrims' progress' of goal achievement with the eventual prize of health, which is itself difficult to define, is not as clear as might be imagined. There is some truth in the assertion that some patients enjoy bad health and that their goal may be seen as treatment or attention, rather than discharge from medical care. Probably these goals are substituted because of inability to achieve them in other areas of life, for example the care and solicitude of the nurses may make up for the absence of love in family life. Alternatively, satisfaction with goals that the medical or nursing staff consider intermediate may be due to the patient's perception of his role.

Reaction by a patient to dependency may be one of frustration in that his normal life pattern is disrupted, or humiliation in that he is unable to function normally together with anxiety about the future. The ways in which the patient deals with these situations vary both between patients and also over time in the same patient. Denial may occur whereby technical help is either not sought or rejected, over-optimism may be displayed with its inevitable disappointments, or exaggerated self-pity and desire for attention may predominate. All these factors will influence the patient's 'goal-setting' and perception of medical and nursing care and make him peculiarly vulnerable to exploitation by those who care for him.

The extent to which this self-role is accepted and the reactions that it produces are inevitably affected by the patient's past experience either as a patient or as an observer of patients. Cultural socialization will have influenced him to respond in different ways and to assign a special meaning and pattern of action to the experience of pain or disability. This cultural variation may produce interpersonal problems when patient and nurse are from different cultures and may give rise to stories of 'uncooperative patients' or 'unfeeling nurses'. A common example of this is the reaction of women to labour pains. On the whole the British woman responds with a stiff upper lip while the woman from one of the Latin races cries, wails and gives marked outward demonstration of every contraction. To the British nurse this is 'making a fuss' and she needs to understand that this is an acceptable form of behaviour in these countries.

NURSE–PATIENT INTERACTION AS SOCIAL EXCHANGE

Sociologists have developed a theory of social exchange to explain some of the ways individuals interact with one another. Cynics argue that little is done in the world from purely altruistic motives but that in every activity there is a reward of some form. Certainly it is necessary to look for the reward when endeavouring to explain why individuals not only take up but continue in the activity of nursing, an occupation which demands unsocial hours, hard physical work, unpleasant sights and sounds, contact with people in their least attractive moments, emotional tension, grief and death. Something must keep nurses at their job and explain why many of them 'would not do anything else'.

Health care within the United Kingdom is organized in such a way that it is frequently considered 'free' because payment does not have to be made at the point of delivery, although this perception is rapidly changing. Since levels of pay for the nursing profession have been increased in recent years, some patients feel that the nurse is caring for them not because she has a vocation but because she is paid to do a job. Other patients do feel that the care they receive is greater than that which is paid for, either by their contributions or by the salary that the nurse receives. Thus there may be an interesting relationship where the nurse may be seen to be the giver of a gift, that of her care, and the patient the receiver without the normal provision for the return of gifts; indeed gifts by patients to nurses are officially frowned on. In fact, the ability to return gifts, such as birthday or Christmas presents, demands an equality of relationship between the giver and the receiver which, during the time that the individual is receiving nursing care, does not exist.

Although the patient may only be in a state of temporary dependence, in the case of the chronic sick, handicapped or dying, the dependence may be permanent. Therefore repayment for nursing care is considered by many to be impossible. It is this inequality of relationship that places nursing in the category of occupations which are considered vocational by the general public and which gives nurses much of their esteem. An effort to restore the balance may be made by the patient by the gift of gratitude.

However, in view of the discussion on the motivation of nurses, it may be that they are repaid in this situation in that the dependence of the patient satisfies the nurse's psychological needs. Nurses themselves tend to indicate that this is the situation and if not prevented may, as already suggested, increase the dependency of the patient or prolong it (the complaint of many patients that in hospital they are not allowed to undertake normal physical activities of which they are quite capable and that the conversation is such that they are reduced to the intellectual level of children is an example of this enforced and increased dependency). Tönnies said (1887): 'What I do for you, I do only as a means to effect your simultaneous, previous or later service for me . . . To get something from you is my end, my service is the means thereto which I naturally contribute unwillingly.' It is probable that this sort of statement throws light on the fact that the care of some classes of patients is seen as less prestigious in the eyes of a society which tends to classify the worth of individuals in relation to the contribution they make to society. It is not difficult to see that the *stigma* of dependency operates most on the old, the chronically sick, the mentally subnormal and those who are unlikely to recover and therefore be in a position where they may be givers in society. Although in the long run most people will experience extreme dependency, society as such does not tolerate such a situation despite the rhetoric of social reformers who talk about the 'caring society' or the 'welfare state'. This stigmatization of the patient may also be perceived by the nurse and result in the care of these patients being considered less prestigious (perhaps the stigma can be said to become attached to those who care for them) and this may also account for nurses who consider their calling a true vocation, for example members of religious orders, particularly focusing their attention on these groups.

Pinker (1971) has described this situation, where the individual is unlikely to be able to repay, as one where the person is perpetually subject to a 'compassion gap'. Furthermore, he points out that the relationship between the giver and the receiver is always inherently an unstable and unequal one and that though gratitude may be used to help restore the balance, because a gift is given first the gratitude may be given with a sense of coercion. Money is the commodity which produces instant equivalence and even the interest paid on money borrowed shows that that lack of equivalence is only temporary. Gratitude is not seen in this light and it is generally agreed that it is more blessed to give than receive.

All this would indicate that the interaction between nurse and patient must inevitably produce feelings of stigma on behalf of the patient and that the satisfaction of needs or the power conveyed to the nurse by the relationship, must in themselves be sufficiently rewarding to enable the interaction to continue. It is interesting that where payment for services is overt, as in the case of private nursing, many nurses express their dislike of the situation, seeing themselves relegated to the role of a servant. Those who do like private nursing usually give as their reason that they have time to do their work properly, to talk to and to get to know the patient. This indicates that the relationship between the nurse and the patient is perhaps less unequal than it may at first seem.

Figure 12 demonstrates this interaction as a form of social exchange, illustrating the goals and the needs of both the patient and the nurse. A '+' sign indicates attributes or skills available and a '−' sign deficiencies that have to be made up if the integrity of the individual is to be maintained and his needs met.

A diagram such as this if added up in terms of '+' or '−' may indicate that there is an imbalance with the nurse in credit and the patient remaining in debt. However, there is no indication as to the strength or depth of any of these factors; if 'weighting' could be carried out the result might be different. Also the nurse may receive other rewards from society such as social esteem and/or social mobility and career advancement; money, although nurses are now paid a more realistic salary, is unlikely to be a major factor, but job security is probably rising in value. Equally, there may be other factors weighing against the patient, in particular the time dimension of the dependency and whether society perceives him as likely to be able to contribute eventually or whether he will remain an economic and social liability. Even this latter situation may be tolerated by society if the person's previous contribution has been large or prestigious, as may be the case for those injured defending their country, although it must be acknowledged that society has a short memory. Other factors affecting perception of worth will be race, age and class.

Frequently, in hospital, patients exercise a degree of care for each other, physically by 'making the early morning tea', psychologically by reassuring and emotional support, and socially by the provision of an ongoing society or group. In providing this mutual aid patients may see themselves to some extent discharging part of their debt to the nurses and to society.

Nurses exhibit a somewhat ambivalent attitude to this

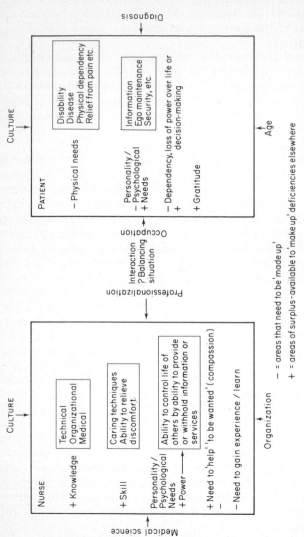

Figure 12. Social exchange: A model of the nurse–patient interaction process and the maintenance of equilibrium.

help given by patients. Often the organization frowns on it (possibly due to legal implications) and although nurses may sometimes ask patients to help they tend to feel guilty for what they perceive as a failure in their ability to cope with the situation themselves. Equally the reluctance, by nurses, to allow patients to continue to carry out self-medication, monitoring or care which they may have given themselves at home may be due to the fact that such behaviour deprives the nurse of satisfaction.

It is an interesting observation that university lecturers often comment on how pleasant the university is in vacations 'without the students' indicating that teaching is not essential to their job satisfaction. Slack periods in the care of the sick are not perceived in the same way, and after a day or two nurses long for more patients to need their care. It would appear that, with few exceptions, patients are essential to the nurse's job satisfaction and this fact may account for the unpopularity amongst most nurses of work in areas such as the operating theatre where interaction with the patient is minimal or absent.

To summarize then, nurse–patient interaction serves to provide the setting in which both parties are able to satisfy their physical and/or sociopsychological needs on an exchange basis. Obviously any specific interaction situation may terminate with a 'debt' on one side or another. However, due to the multiplicity of interaction situations that will occur for each of the participants, these debts may ultimately be cancelled out as interaction incidents are summated. Pinker (1971) asserts that: 'Dependencies of a stigmatizing or humiliating nature are most likely to be avoided when the individual receives aid of a partial nature from a number of providers.' Such observations are important when the organization of care is considered. It may be that the multiplicity of contacts which modern health care demands is not as disfunctional as is commonly believed but that it assists in the lessening of stigma on behalf of the patient, and its value in the relief of stress and anxiety for nurses has already been discussed. Encouraging the patient to take part in setting his own goals, and allowing him as high a level of self-care as is consistent with his ability, will also reduce the stigma of dependency. Such an approach requires changes in the expectations of nurses; no longer will they be doing things 'for' but 'with' patients, who may resent the responsibility of their progress being placed even partially on their shoulders.

References and Further Reading

Altschul, A.T. (1972) *Nurse–Patient Interaction*. Edinburgh: Churchill Livingstone.

Anderson, E.R. (1973) *The Role of the Nurse*. RCN Research Project, **2**, 1. London: RCN

Blau, P.M. (1969) Orientation towards clients in a public welfare agency. *Administrative Science Quarterly*, **5**.

Committee on Nursing (1972) *Briggs Report. Report of the Committee on Nursing*. London: HMSO.

Committee on Senior Nursing Staff Structures (1966) *Salmon Report. Report of the Committee on Senior Nursing Staff Structures*. London: HMSO.

Davis, F. (ed.) (1966) *The Nursing Profession: Five Sociological Essays*. New York: Wiley.

Dingwall, R. & McIntosh, J. (1978) Readings in the Sociology of Nursing. Edinburgh: Churchill Livingstone.

Folta, J. & Deck, E.S. (1979) *A Sociological Framework for Patient Care*. New York: Wiley.

Goffman, E. (1969) *Stigma*. Harmondsworth: Penguin.

Henderson, V. (1962) *Basic Principles of Nursing Care*. Geneva: International Council of Nurses.

Henderson, V. (1967) *The Nature of Nursing*. New York: Macmillan.

Homans, G.C. (1961) *Social Behaviour: Its Elementary Forms*. New York: Harcourt Brace.

Hunt, J.H. & Marks-Maran, D.J. (1980) *Nursing Care Plans: The Nursing Process at Work*. London: HM + M Publishers.

Jones, R.K. & Jones, P. (1975) *Sociology of Medicine*. Chapter 10. London: English Universities Press.

Katz, F.E. (1969) Nurses. In Etzioni, A. (ed.) *The Semi-Professions and their Organization*. New York: Free Press.

King, I.M. (1971) *Toward a Theory for Nursing*. New York: Wiley.

Kratz, C.R. (1979) *The Nursing Process*. London: Baillière Tindall.

McFarlane, J. (1970) *The Proper Study of the Nurse*. RCN Research Project. London: RCN.

Maslow, A.H. (1943) A theory of human motivation. *Psychological Review*, **50**.

Menzies, I.E.P. (1960) A case study in the functioning of social systems as a defense against anxiety. *Human Relations*, **13**.

Merton, R.K. (1957) *Social Theory and Social Structure*. London: Glencoe Press.

Parsons, T. (1964) *The Social System*. London: Glencoé Press.

Pinker, R. (1971) *Social Theory and Social Policy*. London: Heinemann.

Roper, N. (1976) *Clinical Experience in Nursing Education*. Edinburgh: Churchill Livingstone.

Roth, J.A. (1962) The treatment of tuberculosis as a bargaining process. In Rose, A.M. (ed.) *Human Behaviour and Social Processes*. London: Routledge & Kegan Paul.

Roy, C. (1974) Adaptation: a conceptual framework for nursing. *Nursing Outlook*, **18**(3), 42–45.

Timasheff, N.S. (1966) *Sociological Theory — Its Nature and Growth*. New York: Random House.

Tönnies, F. (1887) *Community and Associations* [translated by Loomis, P.] (1955) London: Routledge & Kegan Paul.

Yura, H. & Walsh, M.B. (1978) *The Nursing Process*. New York: Appleton-Century-Crofts.

9 Perceiving the Situation

One of the problems facing the police when interviewing witnesses after a road accident is the fact that honest, well-intentioned individuals may flatly contradict each other when describing the sequel of events. What they perceived in many cases was different to what actually occurred. However: 'If men define situations as real they are real in their consequences' (Thomas and Znaniechi, 1927). Individual perception in a situation is shaped by past experience. This may be direct experience in that the individual has been in a similar position before or it may be indirect in that the situation has been read about, seen on television or been described by friends or relations, and in Western society the part played by mass communications in shaping attitudes and expectations is important.

Mass communications

To a person born in this age of newspapers, radio, television and international postal and telephone services it is difficult to imagine the life of a Britain dependent on pedlars, the stage coach or the annual market, for news of happenings further afield than the immediate neighbourhood. Few of the population in those days could read or write other than their own name and they were so concerned with whether their land would produce enough to live on, or who would be the next Lord of the Manor, that events in other parts of the world were irrelevant.

The press

Large cities such as London had the forerunners of the

present newspapers in the form of broadsheets which were available in coffee houses for those who could read, and most towns employed a crier to inform the populace of major items of interest. Following the Education Acts of the nineteenth century there grew up a large body of people who possessed a degree of skill in the three 'Rs', reading, writing and arithmetic, and at the same time the development of machines meant that newspapers could be produced more cheaply and in larger quantities than before and so began the era of the mass media. Since that time newspapers have increased in circulation, radio has developed and the possession of television is now widespread. Not only are all members of the population able to be 'in touch' with happenings as they occur worldwide, but they are also open to influence by politicians, advertisers, or indeed any agency able to pay for the right of presenting its case.

British newspapers have a long and jealously guarded history of private ownership. This results in policies, shown by the news selected for printing, leader articles and editorials, being under the control of the owners who have to 'make the paper pay'. This freedom of the press is felt by many to be one of the hallmarks of a democratic state and, providing the country's laws such as those of libel or indecency are not violated, there are no restrictions.

However, there are people who feel that this 'freedom' may be open to abuse. When newspapers first began to be widely read every town had its own press and there were few national papers, but over the years there has been a tendency for ownership to become concentrated in the hands of a small number of people. Although the owner leaves the day-to-day running of a newspaper to the editor, obviously he will choose someone who holds similar views to himself and hence the paper is likely to reflect a bias in one or another direction. Some may have a direct link with a political party and hence slant the news, instead of reporting it impartially. Even the advertisements affect public opinion, acting as 'hidden persuaders'.

Sensational reporting or excessive concentration on

trivialities may result from a desire to boost circulation figures rather than to inform. There is a danger that stereotypes will be developed and prejudice reinforced by the way incidents are reported, for example a person's race or colour of skin may be mentioned when it is irrelevant to the issue in question.

Although about 96% of the British populace read a newspaper daily, some minority groups consider that they are not catered for and this has resulted in the development of the 'underground' press which prints small editions of papers covering topics largely ignored by the popular press.

In the United Kingdom editors and journalists writing in papers often see themselves as watchdogs of the government on behalf of the electorate but in some countries the opposite occurs. The press may be in the hands of the government, which, by use of censorship, is able to influence the people and restrict knowledge that might be against its political ideology. It is perhaps true that all papers in the United Kingdom carry a degree of propaganda but because of the variety that exists people select those that appeal to them; where the papers are in government hands no such choice exists.

The role played by magazines and journals is even more difficult to ascertain and certainly they are even more likely to be selected in accordance with the individual's income and social class than newspapers. Their role varies, some are overtly educative in function, others while providing comment on the news may have a marked political bias, while many claim to be purely entertaining.

From the view of the health educationalist it is interesting to note that most magazines catering primarily for women contain sections on 'Care of the baby', 'Dr X's casebook' or 'Consult the nurse'. A health visitor researcher found that many women used these columns as a first-line approach before consulting their doctor. As women's weekly magazines sell between eight and nine million a week, their effect may be considerable.

Television and radio

The development of radio at the turn of the century formed a watershed in communications in that the speed by which news could be disseminated and the distances bridged made them 'mass' in reality. An example of this speed and spread of news is the assertion that within half an hour of the shooting of President Kennedy two out of every three people in the United States knew and within two hours, 90%. During the Second World War radio was used not only to inform but to help maintain morale both in the United Kingdom and, by the use of illicit radio receivers, in the occupied countries. Equally, attempts were made by both sides to use it for propaganda purposes, with limited success.

Following the war, and in face of the development of television, radio still purveys news, entertainment and educational programmes. The development of the transistor has enabled sets to become smaller and more portable, and, associated with the growth of 'pop' music, such a set has become a requirement of all self-respecting teenagers, as a badge of 'youth culture'. The educational use of radio has spread from school programmes to the transmission of teaching for the Open University.

Television, possibly because of its similarity with the cinema, is considered by many to be a primary form of escapism. Certainly some research has shown that the personally or socially deprived are heavy users of television and many of the programmes feed fantasy by portraying high status occupations, glamorous life-styles and exciting situations. Much of the material produced is mentally undemanding, such as light entertainment and drama. However, this is not necessarily either 'wrong' or 'bad'. Television is a leisure-time pursuit, watched when not at work and therefore a matter of personal choice. Rest, relaxation and indeed escapism may be necessary in order to allow the individual a respite before returning to the 'real world'. The danger exists when television becomes a real world. The great hopes held by some that television would provide a major focus of education for the ordinary citizen may not have been realized. However, there is evidence that it may act as a stimulus, illustrated, for example, by the demand for specific books from public libraries after a particular television programme; and the Open University uses television as one of its methods of teaching. There has not been an increase in participation in politics, civic life or even sport as a result of television. The 'narcotizing function' of television is indicated by the fact that many people get vicarious pleasure out of observing events and substitute this for participation. The narcotizing function may also occur over news items; the shock experienced by seeing a famine victim in the living room is rapidly replaced by insensitivity.

The same sort of factors operate politically as with the press. People listen to the programmes that coincide with their views and the failure of politicians to use television to increase their votes has been demonstrated in most recent UK elections. Audience research by the BBC confirms that viewers' attitudes are not changed although some may have been reinforced (Rose, 1966). Instead it appears that party affiliations are brought about by a lengthy period of socialization rather than by the short-term electoral campaign.

Although television can be used educationally both in a formal manner, as with the Open University broadcasts and documentaries, and informally as in the serials portraying the life of a policeman or nurse, there is a danger with the latter type of programme in that only the glamorous aspects of the role may be shown and that 'stereotypes' will be developed.

Nurses have frequently suffered in the hands of television producers, usually being made to appear glamorous and only interested in marrying the doctor. Life on the wards is shown as a mixture of high drama and romance and it is salutory to realize that for some patients admitted to hospital their only information and source of anticipatory socialization comes from such programmes.

Television exists by consent of the Government since the BBC became publicly owned in 1954 and at the same time the Independent Television Authority was granted a licence. The latter depends largely on advertising for its income and these advertisements also reinforce the high status, high life-style as being the norm rather than the exception. The happy smiling mother in a dream kitchen with two intelligent children (boy and girl) and loving husband, obviously earning over £25 000 a year, is portrayed in a way that implies everyone should be like that. Such a portrayal must arouse envy in the less fortunate and may help produce unrealistic consumption patterns. On a visit to the Far East the author saw a television set in the middle of the jungle showing such programmes to the inhabitants of the village. This was their picture of the West. No wonder when such people get to the United Kingdom they are disappointed.

The cinema

At one time most of the dream world to which people escaped was the product of Hollywood. Pre-1939 there were approximately 15 000 000 attendances at the cinema per week but by 1966 this had dropped to 10 000 000. However, recent figures suggest that this fall has ceased and that there may even be a small rise in numbers. The purpose of showing films is commercial, which therefore governs their content. The cult of the film star, now largely supplanted by the pop star, results in changes in fashion, patterns of life-style, language used and may produce or reinforce popular beliefs and prejudice.

The fact that television shows many films originally intended for the cinema means that much of what has already been said about television was first said about the cinema and still applies. However, the social aspect of the cinema means that it is a place where people can meet (and hold hands!) and therefore it has a function quite separate from television. Also since the abolition of censorship, films not deemed suitable for the small screen are able to be shown.

From a sociological point of view the main interest in the mass media is in the interaction between communications and culture. There are various possibilities relating to the attitudes of those who exercise the control. The first is an authoritarian stance so that the communications are seen as the instructions of the ruling class (compare who owns the press). Secondly, it may be viewed as paternalistic, especially as censorship is said to be for the 'protection' of society, or the attitude may be purely commercial: 'if the people want it, it is good'. Many people rebel against all these, wanting a public service with freedom for artists, journalists and those who may be said to be consumers, regardless of the ideology of any specific group.

The danger of mass communication is that it may produce a mass culture which will be primarily passive with artificially created 'wants' and little critical ability. There is a picture of the mass (greatest number of people) all eating the same breakfast cereal, listening to the same pop music and voting for the same party.

Stereotypes

One of the results of the use of mass media is that groups of characteristics are attributed to certain classes of people. A policeman is frequently depicted as being rather fat, with flat feet and a kind heart. Nurses are portrayed as gentle, kind, dressed in a white apron with a becoming cap. Farmers wear corduroy trousers tied with string and a check shirt, and so on. While these images may not be true of the vast majority it is doubtful whether they are actually harmful. More dangerous is the stereotype that occurs related to illness and especially mental illness. From childhood via jokes, the mass media and folklore, the mentally sick person is portrayed as engaging in bizarre behaviour, often dangerous in nature, and is considered not only to act differently from the main population but also to look different. Unlike the attitude to the physically sick person who it is considered cannot help being ill, there tends to be a feeling that because the mentally sick person cannot meet social expectations he is not trying, and because many of the words used in mental illness such as depressed and anxious are used in everyday life there is the feeling that the individual should be able to cope with the situation by his own efforts. Finally, once 'mentally ill' always potentially 'mentally ill' in the eyes of the general population, so that the individual's credibility as a responsible person is lost.

Labelling

In medical practice people are classified according to their signs and symptoms which result in a diagnosis. The effect of *labelling* people in this way is often subtle but nevertheless permeates the perception of most people. One consequence is that the label implies that all people covered by it are alike. This is certainly not true, but if adhered to results in patients being considered as 'neurotics' or 'diabetics' rather than as an individual who happens to have a certain mental or physical state. There is a good deal of evidence to support the idea that illness is socially defined, so that anyone who has had an illness associated with the heart is considered unable to indulge in exercise or hard work despite the actual physiological state, and to tell someone that he has high blood pressure may alter his life-style for the rest of his life. Absence from work for more than a few days has to be legitimized by a doctor and this need for his agreement with the label 'ill' can cause problems when no objective disease process is present, yet the individual 'feels' or 'acts as' ill.

Health is perceived by society as a positive goal, hence the moral condemnation of action which obviously flaunts the chances of 'keeping well'. This may even be considered as deviant behaviour. The change in attitude towards people who smoke, overeat, drink excessively and so on reflects this perception that people should avoid hazards to health. Debates over abortion, use of drugs, noise, pollution of the air and many other issues are influenced largely by considerations of their impact on the health of the population. Part of the anxiety and, in some cases, delay in a patient reporting symptoms to a doctor is due to the fear of sickness and its impact on normal functioning.

STIGMA

Individuals who bear outward signs of their physical condition, those with skin lesions, the deformed and disabled are stigmatized by society, that is, they are treated differently. The averted glance, the movement away from physical contact, and the whispered remark all serve to demonstrate that the individual is 'different' and does not fit into society's perception of an acceptable person. This stigmatization also occurs in relation to the patient with mental illness and may also be attached to those whom society sees as of little worth such as the old, the drug addict or alcoholic. In the last five years the upsurge in AIDS (acquired immune deficiency syndrome) has demonstrated to a bizarre degree the effects of stigma, with people being afraid to be near a person with such a diagnosis let alone touch them. There appears to be a reaction in society similar to that reserved for lepers in a previous age.

Many writers have commented that some patients get very little attention from nurses other than that which is absolutely essential for their care, while others appear frequently to have a group of nurses around their bed. These latter patients were the ones classed by nurses as 'good' and Stockwell (1972) found that these patients were the ones that:

'Were able to communicate readily with the nurses.
Knew the nurses' names.
Were able to laugh and joke with the nurses.
Cooperated in being helped to get well and expressed determination to do so.'

(It is interesting that only the last point is mentioned in the definition of the 'patient role', see page 40.) The least popular patients were those who either grumbled or demanded attention, or those whom the nurses, for various reasons, felt should not be in hospital or in that specific ward. (In an acute general ward this particularly applied to any patient with psychiatric symptoms.)

Finally, another group of patients was identified who, while neither rated popular nor unpopular, nevertheless had little verbal contact with the nurses. This could have been from choice, but Stockwell, by virtue of her observations, felt it was largely because they felt unable to initiate conversation with the nurse, and the nurse made no effort to do so.

This, and other studies, indicate that nurses had little insight into the possible reasons for 'good' or 'bad' behaviour. Viguers (1959) observed: 'It is the "impossible" patient who may need most attention and care. The easy thing is to try and avoid the patient who makes unreasonable demands, fails to follow instructions and seems unappreciative, whatever is done for him, but if we can understand some of the emotional aspects of being hospitalized, we can more readily give the difficult patient the added care and attention he is asking for and needs.' Another comment: 'A difficult patient often is described as demanding, uncooperative to treatment, unappreciative or generally unlikeable. Actually a difficult patient is one whose needs are not met — emotional, physical, or both.' Once a patient has been labelled as difficult or uncooperative he will be treated as such and a vicious circle of self-fulfilling prophecy will result.

Nursing textbooks and teaching insist that all patients must be treated alike and a lot has been said and written in other spheres of life about the problem of inequality and discrimination, but to treat all patients alike may produce inequalities because of the unequal level of need. Benn and Peters (1965) assert that: 'A just decision regarding action (in their case public administration) includes the necessity of differences in treatment, providing these differences can be justified by differences in attitude or condition and that the differences in treatment are in a loose sense proportionate.' What is required, they say, is: 'Impartiality — the principle that discrimination must be grounded on relevant differences. Otherwise men stand equal.' This should be the principle behind the planning and delivery of patient care. If 'patient centred', then individual differences of need will be appreciated and care will not be a matter of routine but consist in meeting those needs in an individual manner: some patients will require more time and skill than others and provided that there is 'impartiality' this will be appropriate.

THE NURSE'S PERCEPTION

The nurse also defines the situation in which she finds herself and this initially will depend on her motivation to nurse and her perception of the nurse's role. These factors have already been discussed (see Chapter 4) but may be briefly repeated. A nurse perceiving any specific situation relating to a patient may see it as one where her place is to provide physical care which the patient is unable to carry out himself; it may be viewed as a situation in which a technique may be performed with skill or possibly practised for the first time: the patient may be viewed as an interesting example of a certain disease which may be studied, or seen as an individual who needs recognition as such with appropriate support (emotional, intellectual, spiritual, physical) to maintain his dignity. These perceptions are not necessarily mutually exclusive and fortunate indeed is the patient who finds the nurse who is able to sustain and fulfil these aspects of her role, instrumental and expressive, simultaneously.

Obviously the neophyte nurse's original perception of the nurse's role and possibly her subsequent motivation will be affected by the way in which she is socialized into that role and therefore the attitudes of her teachers. It is not without cause that hospitals develop a reputation for a particular style of nursing based on their selection of new entrants to nursing and subsequent socialization and training.

Work has been done to assess the personality traits of nursing students both in the United States and the United

Kingom, using Edwards Personal Preference Schedule (Appendix I) as a research instrument (Singh, 1972). This is a forced choice personality inventory which provides measures on fifteen manifest need or personality characteristics. It was found that the English nursing student sample differed significantly from the Edwards norm group on ten of the fifteen personality needs. Using these findings, Singh described the average English student nurse as follows:

> She has considerable need for living in an organized and self-disciplined fashion. She also gains satisfaction from neatness and from her awareness of details. She has little interest in knowing about what others think, or in exhibiting real need to take an independent stand.

> She is also more non-authoritarian than authoritarian in her need to conform to the conventional and the traditional, in her more frequent identification with liberal rather than conservative thinking. In the area of human relations and social endeavours, she has no great need to develop intimate relationships and friendships or to form strong attachments to particular others, but she is strongly motivated by a need to help and serve others. She has also no desire to assume responsibility or to attempt to guide or direct the efforts of others. She also has considerable need for heterosexual activities.

> She is persistent and not easily distracted either from immediate tasks or remote goals: this represents an investment in ritualized performance rather than interest in accomplishing and achieving goals, in deriving satisfaction from the application of effort and energy or in acquiring recognition.

> The English student shows little interest in power, prestige and in having control over others, but at the same time is critical, resentful and less willing to be dependent on or to defer to others.

The English sample scored higher on the need for autonomy

and lower on the needs for intraception and dominance than an American hospital diploma senior student nurse sample. These findings are of interest as they indicate that while the English nurse has a strong need to help and serve others she does not feel the need to develop strong relationships with them and is less likely to analyse the feelings and motives of others in an attempt to understand how they feel. Unfortunately, as the studies of both the American and English students were done when they were in their third year of training, it is impossible to determine how much these needs had been affected by training.

Certainly the conventional British training for nurses emphasized that nurses should not become emotionally involved with patients, and the typical American training emphasized the need to understand, to talk to and empathize with the patient. Possibly the tendency to stress efficient task performance, including those which are mainly traditional in origin and have little value for the patient, is the result of training rather than original characteristics. Recent years have witnessed a gradual change in this traditional 'non-involvement' approach and nurses are now encouraged to empathize and treat the patient as an individual, realizing that such a relationship may be painful. Such an approach requires an adequate support system for nurses to allow them to express their own anxieties and stress. This is sometimes provided by the nurses' peers, sometimes by senior nursing staff, especially nurse tutors, and, in a few cases, by trained counsellors.

Although some able nurses leave the clinical field to enter administration in order to progress in their career and to receive greater financial reward, some would prefer not to fill these posts. If the profile of the English nurse as portrayed by Singh is accurate, this may be true, as he indicates a low need for power prestige and control over others. However, if a reading of the nursing press or attendance at professional meetings is a guide, there are a considerable number of the profession who do not fit this part of the profile. Patients certainly often comment on the 'bossiness' of the nurses and there is little doubt that they frequently wield considerable power, although unconscious of the fact.

COMMUNICATIONS, VERBAL AND NON-VERBAL

Discussions with student nurses reveal that they are not aware of the way in which they withhold information from patients (sometimes because they do not possess it themselves but often because they do not realize its importance to the patient), or the fact that the patient is rarely consulted about quite small matters such as whether the window should be opened or closed, number of blankets, and so on — all often seen by patients as evidence of power. What is worse to the patient is that this power is, to use Etzioni's term, coercive, as they have little or no redress. A letter in *The Nursing Times* (Nemo, 1973) from a patient describing her experience in hospital demonstrates this feeling of powerlessness related to a longing for a cup of tea, and another patient (a business executive) stated that patients are forced into a state of submission; 'When I was asked to walk around my room wearing only that humble hospital gown, open the length of the back, in the presence of personnel my ego was so deflated I couldn't even protest; they had me cowed all the time I was in the hospital.'

One of the ways in which a nurse may maintain power over a patient is by the use of her knowledge as most patients are naïve in respect of medical conditions and terms. This is also an area where there is a real threat to their very existence and therefore those who understand the mysteries of life and death, such as doctors and nurses, may use this to their own ends. Nurses may be tempted to do so because it is the only area where they have power. In many ward situations doctors use their knowledge to exercise power over the ward sister; the ward sister uses her knowledge to exercise power over the nurses and so the nurse completes the chain by withholding from the patients knowledge which they may wish to have. To be fair to nurses, in many cases they may not realize what they are doing, their attitudes stemming from the ward ethos of restricting information. Of course there are patients who do not wish to know what is the matter with them or details of their treatment or progress. In this case the nurse has no power over them because knowledge is only power if it is desired by the person deprived of it.

Although a great deal is said and written about the lack of understanding on the part of the patient which implies that it is related to lack of knowledge or intelligence, it frequently occurs that the knowledgeable and intelligent patient is also 'left in the dark'. Staff assume that such a patient will automatically know what is happening, why treatment is given and what is expected, when in fact this may not be the situation. It is commonplace to assert that 'a little knowledge is a dangerous thing' but sometimes 'a lot is even worse' and anxiety may be increased because of an understanding of possible complications, potential dangers or long-term implications.

One of the difficulties experienced by students in learning how to talk to patients is that they are rarely able to observe the skilled nurse at work. Indeed there is resistance to any suggestion that a third person should be present, 'No-one can teach you how to form a relationship, it is personal. If anyone were there it would erect a barrier.' Secondly the nurse has no way of assessing whether her reaction with the patient is valuable in any way other than social contact.

This need to help nurses 'listen and talk' has been demonstrated by Dr Frances Reiter of New York in tests administered during a series of lectures and discussions on communications (1966). A test was conducted in the form of role play and indicated that communication with the patient was either in the form of instructions or social chat, rarely did the nurses obtain vital social information or commence the building of a relationship which might later be invaluable.

The nurse practitioners themselves came to realize that no matter how well-intentioned, their conversations had not been directed to the patient's problem, . . . and often failed to evoke even a feeling of trust. The nurses identified many of their conversations as being of a suppressive, coercive or persuasive nature and recognized that their conversations had concentrated the focus of attention on the physical–therapeutic need almost to the exclusion of the patient's equally imperative emotional need. They identified very few conversations in which they encouraged patient autonomy or initiative, and appreciation of power as perceived by the patient must be realised so that it can be used sparingly or not at all, so that patients feel a greater degree of self-determination.

EMBARRASSMENT

One of the factors that acts as a barrier to easy interaction and which affects both staff and patient is the phenomenon called embarrassment. Goffman (1956) states that embarrassment is the result of 'disconfirmation of the self-image presented in an encounter'. The image and role presented to the other individual in any interaction situation must be acccepted and the appropriate responses given to maintain that role. Both parties must have consensus as to their position and roles so that interaction may take place, with a 'meshing' of expectations and responses. However, such a meshing may not occur if there is a high degree of social anxiety, if the rules of the situation (etiquette) are not known by all parties, if the presentation of one or more roles lacks authenticity and competence or if either of the individuals is low in self-esteem. If such a situation develops, the discomfort produced may be of so great an intensity that interaction has to cease temporarily while a new level of concensus is worked out.

Such an experience is by no means confined to the nurse–patient situation but is experienced in many walks of life where one or more of the interacting individuals is ignorant of the expectations of the situation. However, the nurse–patient situation is particularly vulnerable to embarrassment in that not only are new rules of etiquette to be learned by the patient but many firmly established rules have to be broken, many of which carry with them deeply entrenched social taboos such as exposure of private parts of the body and discussion of matters which are normally repressed. Such a situation may produce extreme social anxiety and the high emotional arousal on the part of the patient can be reduced by tact and skill on behalf of the nurse as the other interacting member. Unfortunately this skill has to be learned and requires a stable level of self-esteem and a high degree of empathy; meanwhile such encounters frequently occur between the junior nurse and the patient. The student nurse therefore is battling with the problem of developing her own mature self-image and at the same time is learning technical skills which she may be using on the patient for the first time. The image she presents to the patient may lack the authenticity needed to reassure the patient that the interaction is valid and that the situation is under control. Meanwhile the student nurse may feel totally unable to cope with both her own conflicting emotions and lack of skill and therefore be unable to help the patient to adjust to this new situation.

Menzies (1960) has graphically described how the nurse endeavours to reduce this social anxiety by depersonalizing her service to the patient, seeing him as an object, thus reducing the intensity of the contact by detachment and denial of feelings. Further, the responsibility of the outcome of the interaction is reduced by removal of the need to make decisions by ritual task performance, spreading the responsibility for care of the patient, checks and counter-checks and the avoidance of innovations.

Since this study, medical science has continued to progress in such a way that many of the ritualized task performances are now inappropriate and the care of the patient has polarized into either intensive personal care requiring a high degree of skill or into hotel care with transitory nursing activity. In the first case the nurses must therefore be able to sustain close and continuous contact with the patient during the crisis period of the illness, carrying out highly skilful activities. The danger of this situation is that the performance of the skilled tasks may provide the excuse for the lack of interaction with the patient. Such patients, by nature of their physical condition, if conscious, need a high degree of reassurance. At such a time the conventional 'you'll be all right' and the performance of tasks with little or no explanation is anything but reassuring. No one would suggest that the nurse should spend time talking to the patient when what he needs primarily is the administration of oxygen, but once that has been done then time should be taken to explain the 'why' and 'how' of the situation and an effort made to appreciate how the patient perceives his condition.

At the other end of the scale the patient who needs little nursing care but is able to carry out most of his own requirements needs the opportunity to discuss his condition, hopes and fears. As this opportunity may not arise during a conventional nursing situation, conscious effort must be made by the nurse to make such a communication situation possible. The high regard for task performance and the fear of being unable to cope with topics that may be raised during such a conversation mean that it is rarely allowed to develop.

Altschul (1972), studying nurse–patient interaction in the psychiatric field, found that even in an area where such interaction might be considered to have high priority the patients felt that the nurses only had time to talk to the physically ill and the nurses supported this view, as illustrated by the following quotation:

> *Patient:* Now they (the nurses) can't talk to the patients because their schedule is too tight, they have no time because of Mr X (who was physically ill). If he is in bed he gets more attention than those who are fit and on the mend.

Organizational factors therefore need to be overhauled so that nurses are allowed to develop closer relationships with patients. This necessitates less movement of staff, greater acceptance of the idea that 'talking is working' and less emphasis on task performance. The increased use of nursing histories, assessment of need, planning of care and evaluation of results as required in the 'nursing process' is a welcome step towards these aims, although even here the completion of the appropriate forms may become an end in itself rather than a means to better nurse–patient interaction.

EMPATHY

To enable meaningful communication to take place the nurse not only requires the appropriate areas of knowledge but must possess empathy. Many would argue that empathy is not something that can be learned but is a basic psychological trait, and others would question the value of the skill, seeing it as a non-scientific, uncontrolled emotional response of questionable value in nursing.

In that empathy cannot occur in a state of self-consciousness, the difficulty of teaching this activity can be readily seen. However, it is possible to develop this attitude of receptiveness and availability, what has been described as 'making room' with oneself. Not only does the empathizer withdraw his attention from himself but turns to the other person the whole of himself. It has been described as 'listening with the third ear'.

The commencement of such activity is usually in a response to cues emanating from the other person. These are frequently non-verbal and subtle so that the recipient is often unaware of receiving them. In the first stage of the activity the empathizer then 'steps into the other man's shoes'. This form of identification is temporary, effective and intuitive. Described as: 'I imagine to myself what another man is at this very moment wishing, feeling, perceiving, thinking, and not as a detached content but in his very reality, this is, as a living process in this man' (Baber, 1957). Second, the empathizer experiences an inner response to the internalized content and may react emotionally or physically.

At this stage it is as if the empathizer's ego had split, with the one part he vicariously shares the other's experience, but with the other he observes it. 'To sense the client's private world as if it were your own, but without ever losing the "as if" quality — this is empathy' (Rogers, 1957). The third stage is detachment and return or re-entry into the empathizer's own world. He backs away from the identification and subjective involvement and scrutinizes the activity, critically testing it against the reality of his own experience.

The concept of empathy involves the idea of movement — 'a standing where he stands' and this is obviously easier if the empathizer has been there in reality. Previous experience therefore may facilitate or hinder the activity of empathy. The nurse may not wish to experience empathy or indeed see it as of value. Emphasis on task performance, the consideration of the patient only as someone to whom something has to be done or even someone to be studied, will hinder empathy. However, in a view of nursing as 'helping another person', knowledge of the patient's perspective is essential and empathy valued as a means of gaining such knowledge.

Nurses, if encouraged to study their relationship with patients, can be made aware of the constant tensions that exist in the patient's world and can be shown how, by understanding any of these tensions, sense can be made of their own and the patient's interactive experience. Often the spark of understanding can be lit by reading patients' accounts of their experiences in hospital and the skilful teacher may be able to draw an analogy between the nurse's experiences as a child and those of the dependent patient. Guided introspection and a stimulated imagination will both assist the nurse in her task of 'taking on the reality of the patient'.

Sociologists often use the term 'role-taking' to indicate this activity and it can develop from 'subjective' experience with similar roles, and 'objective' experience in observing others in these roles. However, 'role-taking' is a metaphor: 'We do not and cannot literally "take" another's role. When we "project" ourselves into another's situation and imagine how we would feel, we are sometimes impressed by the intensity and realism of our own feelings but these feelings are ours, not his and the accuracy of our role-taking remains uncertain.' (McCall and Simmons, 1971)

One of the problems associated with the teaching of skills which may discourage empathy is the view, still held by many nurses, that it is bad to get 'involved' with the patient. There is a fairly commonly held view that it is only by being detached that the nurse can carry out tasks for the patient which may be embarrassing if viewed in the context of the culture, may be unpleasant and/or offensive to the nurse, or are painful for the patient. Equally, detachment may be seen as the hallmark of professionalism, so that the nurse may deliberately dampen any sense of warmth or tenderness and aim at cold efficiency. In social work a writer comments: 'Caseworkers, as professionals, were expected to relate to the client in a detached, emotionally neutral manner. The control of emotional effect in relationship with clients is meant to encourage impartial service and to ensure that the practitioner's judgement is guided by reason rather than emotion.' (Scott, 1966) It is the need to apply reasonable judgement that requires the next stage in empathy. Indeed it is the third stage of empathy, the withdrawal and critical scrutiny of the situation, that distinguishes the empathy used in a clinical situation from that which occurs spontaneously in everyday life and it is this ability to withdraw that is required in involvement with patients. There is therefore a need to develop self-awareness amongst the students so that many have greater insight into their own anxieties and behaviour as well as those of their patients.

It is probably true that the patients' expectations of the nurse are related to an unrealistic assessment of her individual resources and capabilities, physical, educational and managerial, and that the patient needs to realize that only the exceptional personality is able 'to be all things to all men'. As already pointed out, it is important for roles to synchronize: 'A doctor cannot act as a doctor unless the patient acts like a patient.' However, there are no courses in how to become a patient and little in the mass media which portrays the role realistically. As already mentioned, some education may be given via women's magazines or the *Family Doctor* booklets, but of necessity these can only reach a very limited audience. A television programme stripped of the drama, glamour and love interest would probably have low viewing figures. Nevertheless, there is a need for such a programme to produce greater understanding.

SHARED PERCEPTIONS

One of the factors that is paramount in any analysis of nursing is the awareness that nursing necessitates a face-to-face interaction situation. King (1971) has demonstrated this by the model shown in Figure 13. She states that, 'the nursing process is a series of acts which connate action, reaction and interaction and that transaction follows when a reciprocal relationship is established between nurse and patient participating in definition of the goal to be achieved.' The fact that the patient is now always able to participate in this model is appreciated and it is acknowledged that transaction in this case is not possible. A 'working *consensus*' is necessary to enable interaction to take place.

In this model both nurse and patient are looking at the situation but naturally their perceptions may be different. For example, the patient may think that following orthopaedic surgery the leg should be kept quite still to

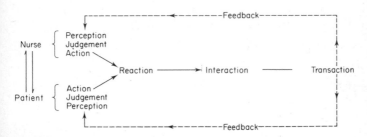

Figure 13. Interaction situation. *Source*: King (1971).

prevent pain, while the nurse may thing that quadriceps muscle exercises will be beneficial; each will act appropriately and deadlock may occur. However, if both realize that the other is seeing the situation differently, the reactions to the proposed action of each will result in communication and interaction, with an appropriate change in the actions of one or possibly a compromise. For example, the patient may be given analgesics to relieve the discomfort, which will encourage performance of the exercises. This approach emphasizes the interpersonal relationship between patient and nurse, the importance of perception, the fact that nurse and patient can contact each other, but for value to be produced by this contact a transaction needs to take place. The importance of perception in this model must be stressed, for if the nurse, using her own standards, perceives the patient as 'making a fuss', she will use that as the basis of her actions regardless of whether or not the patient's behaviour can be explained by medical, psychological, or cultural facts. Equally, a patient who perceives a nurse as 'too bossy' will hesitate to ask for needed care even though the nurse's attitude of harassment is purely one of habit and not due to overwork.

King (1971) used the model shown in Figure 14 to demonstrate the factors determining perception, and this can be applied to both the nurse and the patient but, as has already been discussed, the area X of the two individuals may not coincide.

References and Further Reading

Altschul, A.T. (1972) *Nurse–Patient Interaction*. Edinburgh: Churchill Livingstone.

Argyle, M. (1969) *Social Interaction*. London: Methuen.

Baber, M. (1957) Distance and relation. *Psychiatry*. London: May.

Benn, S.I. & Peters, R.S. (1965) *Some Principles and the Democratic State*. London: Allen & Unwin.

Brown, E.L. (1966). Nursing and patient care. In Davis, F. (ed.) *The Nursing Profession. Five Sociological Essays*. New York: Wiley.

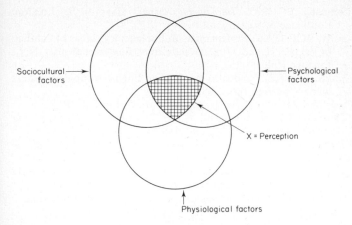

Figure 14. Factors determining perception. *Source*: King (1971).

Burnard, P. (1985) *Learning Human Skills. A Guide for the Nurse*. London: Heinemann Medical Books.

Cartwright, A. (1964) *Human Relations and Hospital Care*. London: Routledge & Kegan Paul.

Goffman, E. (1956) Embarrassment and social organization. *American Journal of Sociology*, **62**.

Halloran, J. (ed.) (1970) *The Effects of Television*. London: Panther.

Hoggart, R. (1977) *The Uses of Literacy*. Harmondsworth: Pelican.

King, I.M. (1971) *Toward a Theory for Nursing*. New York: Wiley.

McCall, G.J. & Simmons, J.L. (1971) The Dynamics of interactions. In Thompson, K. & Tunstall, J. (eds.) *Sociological Perspectives*. Harmondsworth: Penguin.

Menzies, I.E.P. (1960) A case study in the functioning of social systems as a defence against anxiety. *Human Relations*, **13**.

Nemo (1973) Tender loving care. *Nursing Times*, **69**, 29.

Reiter, F. (1966) The nurse clinician. *American Journal of Nursing*, **66**, 2.

Rogers, C.R. (1957) The necessary and sufficient conditions of therapeutic personality change. *Journal of Consulting Psychology*, **31**.

Rose, A.M. (ed.) (1966) *Human Behaviour and Social Processes*. London: Routledge & Kegan Paul.

Scotson, J. (1975) *Introducing Society.* Chapter 9. London: Routledge & Kegan Paul.

Scott, W.R. (1966) Professionals in bureaucracy: areas of conflict. In Volmer, H. (ed.) *Professionalization.* Englewood Cliffs, N.J.: Prentice Hall.

Singh, A. (1972) Personality needs of an English sample of student nurses. *Nursing Times,* **68,** 12.

Stockwell, F. (1972) *The Unpopular Patient.* London: RCN.

Thomas, W.I. & Znaniechi, F. (1927) *Primitive Behaviour: The Polish Peasant in Europe and America.* New York: Denver.

Tschudin, V. (1982) *Counselling Skills for Nurses.* London: Baillière Tindall.

Viguers, R.T. (1959) Be kind to impossible patients — they're scared. *The Modern Hospital,* **92,** 1.

Williams, R. (1963) *Communications.* Harmondsworth: Pelican.

10 Life Events and Illness

It is common for the growth and development of a baby to be marked by 'milestones'. These are significant events such as the first smile, sitting up, crawling and so on. This marking of significant occurrences is not restricted to the infant and the first day at school; puberty, starting work, coming of age, marriage, retirement are also life events which mark a significant change in the role of the individual in society — a status passage (Rahe, 1972). Prior to each of these events there is normally a period of anticipatory socialization; mother plays at being at school with the four-year-old, marriage is preceded by courtship and retirement may be prepared for by special evening classes or the development of new interests. Despite this preparation and the *rites de passage* that accompany it, the passage from one role state to another is a crisis point in the life of the individual and things are never the same afterwards. Not only have the rights and duties of the individual changed but so has his self-image. In some cases, as for example the single girl now perceived both in her own eyes and that of society as a married woman, the change may be both desired and welcomed. In other situations, and retirement is a likely case, the change may have been unwelcome, resisted and not fully accepted. In both cases there will be an emotional response to the change and this may be one of joy, interest or even excitement; alternatively it may be one of fear, anxiety, boredom, alienation or anomie.

STRESS

It is a well-established fact that emotional states may bring about physiological changes and the part that stress may play in illness is increasingly appreciated. Two studies by nurses (Hayward, 1974; Boore, 1978) have demonstrated the relationship between the pain experienced postoperatively by patients and the level of stress engendered by lack of information about their condition.

Life events as described may therefore precipitate illness episodes. The newly married woman may present with an exacerbation of ulcerative colitis or the newly retired with depression. Psychiatric nurses will be well aware that psychiatric disorder may make its presence obvious at the time of a period of stress following a life event. However, not all people react in the same way to life events so there must be other factors which, added together, produce stress of a magnitude which will precipitate illness. For example, the newly married couple who move to a large city from a small country community may find themselves under a good deal of stress if they have housing problems and financial difficulties and no longer have the support of the community in which they were previously integrated. Even so, some couples in a similar situation will survive these stresses with apparently little ill effect so that other factors (? genetic) may also play a part. Nevertheless, much mental illness is the result of the problems of living and some is socially defined; behaviour that is contrary to the expectations of a specific society has to be explained. If against society's norms, as made explicit in the legal system, this deviance may be dealt with by some form of punishment as an attempt is made to suppress it. However, some deviant forms of behaviour are not wrong, i.e. not contrary to society's norms, but different. Toleration of this difference usually depends on the degree it affects other people, and is frequently linked with social class. The professor or the duchess may be affectionately regarded as eccentric while the dustman or shopgirl may be classified as mad. Although the line drawn between the eccentric professor and the dustman defined as mentally ill may be blurred, yet the first is tolerated and the second may be rejected and excluded from society.

BEREAVEMENT

The death of a partner or even a friend causes a change in role and indeed in self-perception. The widow is no longer a wife, one area of interaction has ceased and in many cases the whole reason for living may appear to have disappeared.

This loss of meaning for life has a marked effect on illness and indeed on the mortality patterns of bereaved persons. Studies show that within the first year of bereavement mortality rates for the bereaved are higher than for those of the general population (this includes suicide rates which are also higher). After twelve months the rates fall sharply, possibly indicating that a new meaning for life has been found.

Reaction to bereavement may be one of denial as the person left tries to keep everything the same; it may be inhibited grief or it may be outward grief and mourning. If the death was the culmination of a period of dying, then the bereaved person may have commenced grieving prior to the death actually taking place. This may be a type of anticipatory socialization in the role of the bereaved. A similar feeling of loss may occur in the individual whose marriage breaks down and ends in divorce and even in some cases in the person admitted to hospital. In all cases there is a loss of roles and a separation from signficant others. This loss may initially produce a sense of shock and a sense of unreality, the individual may exhibit an air of self-confidence and even state that 'it was all for the best'. This stage is then replaced by a feeling of sadness, hopelessness and helplessness, often accompanied by a sense either of guilt at not preventing the occurrence or of anger against the circumstances that have produced the loss. Such an individual may become quiet and withdrawn, not participating in everyday activities. This stage is frequently accompanied by physical symptoms such as insomnia, loss of appetite, indigestion, constipation and headaches. Finally there is a gradual acceptance of the situation as socialization into the new role in the community occurs.

DYING

Loss and separation are not feelings confined to the bereaved but are also experienced by the dying. Although few healthy adults give much though to their own deaths, the chronically ill or aged may begin to realize that they are nearing the end of the road of life and that death is a reality. Part of this lack of thought about death is due to 'taboo' that has been imposed by society in the United Kingdom on the subject. Several writers have expressed the opinion that death has replaced sex as the unmentioned topic.

As a result of this there is a marked reluctance on the part of all concerned, doctors, nurses and relatives, to telling a patient that he is dying. This secrecy frequently results in a breakdown in communication between those 'in the know' and those in ignorance. It is particularly unfortunate when this occurs between relatives such as husband and wife, who, at a time when they need mutual support and help, are separated by a barrier of unshared knowledge. The process of dying has been described as a 'trajectory' (Glaser and Strauss, 1965), that is the path made by an object moving under a given force, which has duration and shape (it can be plotted as a graph). The critical phases in this process are:

1. The patient is defined as dying.
2. Staff and family make preparations for the death; the patient may also do this if he is aware of his condition.
3. There is a period of waiting when 'nothing can be done' which may last hours, days, weeks or even months.
4. The terminal phase and last hours will approach.
5. A 'death wake' may occur.
6. Death — legally certified and publicly pronounced.

When the individual realizes he is dying he will also commence to experience the 'loss' of social roles and relationships. Inevitably future plans become meaningless and there may be initially resistance to this as the patient tries to put off the 'social death' which is the forerunner of physiological death. One of the features of hospices and nurses specially prepared to care for the dying patient at home is that in the care they give this social death is postponed as long as possible. Efficient use of drugs controls pain, nausea and other unpleasant physiological symptoms so that the patient may be able to stay at home and is capable of talking to relatives and acting 'as himself' for as long as possible. Fear of death may be the fear of the unknown or the fear of loss of dignity due to pain, nausea and breathlessness. A fear of the actual passage from life to death is frequently less intense as those who believe in an after-life see it as a status passage while those who do not should have nothing to fear.

The nurse's perception of death has altered with the increase in machinery which can apparently prolong life. The doctor's role is to cure and many commentators have noted that once cure becomes unlikely their interest in the patient may be lost (patients have also commented on the fact that they may be ignored by a previously attentive consultant). Despite this, the nurse still has to care for this patient and this attitude of the doctor may affect her perception also. Apart from those institutions that specialize in the care of the dying, the tendency is to 'get the patient home' to die; this may in fact be what the patient and his relatives desire. If, however, the patient remains in hospital, then although he may not be neglected physically he may be ignored except when care is being carried out. Hinton (1967) has noted the loneliness of the dying and feels that many nurses, taking their cue from the doctor, see the patient who dies as evidence of failure on their part. Failure is always painful and hence one way to deal with it is to pretend it has not happened and this cannot be done if close contact is maintained with the evidence. This denial of the facts may lead other doctors and nurses to 'strive officiously to keep the patient alive', denying him the right to die peacefully and with dignity. Western society has produced a taboo on the subject of death and dying and nurses are therefore influenced by this conspiracy of silence, as well as by the attitude of the medical profession, and the distress of the relatives. The age of the patient, especially if near to that of the nurse, may also affect the nurse's perception as to whether dying is 'the proper thing to do' for that specific individual. Fear that they may be unable to cope with the patient's questions may limit the conversation that nurses allow to develop and so the patient may once again feel 'shut out' as the nurse acts in a way which appears to deny the reality of death.

The way in which other patients are protected from the death of a fellow patient is another aspect of society's denial of death. Screens may be drawn to prevent the sight of the body being moved and lies may be told regarding the dead person's transfer to another unit. This denial continues with the terminology used — 'passed away', 'at rest' and 'funeral parlours' or 'rest homes' to describe undertakers' premises.

The ceremony of disposing of the dead person, funeral or cremation, is an important *rites de passage* and is often helpful to the bereaved. It provides an opportunity for friends and relations to demonstrate the 'worthiness' of the dead person and their support and 'social solidarity' with those left. Although, as with all other status changes, society acknowledges that it takes time to get used to the new role, adaptation is expected to take place following the ceremony marking the change and it is at this stage that the bereaved person is frequently left alone and therefore finds it difficult to return to normal social life.

SOCIAL FACTS AND ILLNESS

Despite the fact that illness is defined medically, there is a degree of consensus that much of it may be caused or at any rate precipitated by social factors. Pollution of the environment, water, air, and food, is an obvious example, but so is the relationship, not completely understood, between social class and specific diseases. This relationship is not always clear or indeed causal. Although smoking and carcinoma of the lung have been shown to be linked, it is still not certain whether there is a third factor, for example the genetic makeup of the individual, or personality which makes the person more likely to get cancer. This is not to say that correlations of this type are not important or that the breaking of one of the links, for example smoking, would not lead to improved health for the individual and be economically advantageous for the community.

Stress-related diseases, such as gastric ulcer, coronary heart disease, high blood pressure, and some forms of mental illness, are obviously linked to society and the way in which it functions. The way in which some individuals succumb to stress while others appear to be able to support it without illness may be due to the fact that the latter have support mechanisms in society such as family, friends, or social approval and status which the others lack. This, coupled with the aforementioned genetic and physiological variations, needs more study.

It was a major step forward in the prevention of disease when John Snow took the handle of the Broad Street pump in London and halted the spread of cholera. The realization that society can play a part in both causing and preventing a breakdown in health may not be so dramatic but is no doubt of equal value.

References and Further Reading

Anderson, J.L., Cartwright, A. & Hockey, L. (1973) *Life Before Death*. London: Routledge & Kegan Paul.

Boore, J. (1978) *Prescription for Recovery*. London: RCN.

Brown, G.W. (1976) Social causes of disease. In Tuckett, D. (ed.) *An Introduction to Medical Sociology*. London: Tavistock.

Cartwright, A., Hockey, L. & Anderson, J.L. (1973) *Life before Death*. London: Routledge & Kegan Paul.

Glaser, B.G. & Strauss, A.L. (1965) *Awareness of Dying*. Chicago: Aldine.

Glaser, B.G. & Strauss, A.L. (1968) *Time For Dying*. Chicago: Aldine.

Hayward, J. (1974) *Information: A Prescription Against Pain*. RCN Research Series, **2**, 5. London: RCN.

Hinton, J.M. (1967) *Dying*. Harmondsworth: Pelican.

Jones, R.K. & Jones, P. (1975) *Sociology in Medicine*, Chapter 7. London: English Universities Press.

Kubler-Ross, E. (1970) *On Death and Dying*. New York: Macmillan.

Rahe, R.H. (1972) Subjects' recent life changes and their near-future illness reports. In Roy, C. (ed.) (1974) *Conceptual Models For Nursing Practice*. New York: Appleton-Century-Crofts.

Speck, P. (1978) *Loss and Grief in Medicine*. London: Baillière Tindall.

Sudnow, D. (1967) *Passing On: The Social Organization of Dying*. Englewood Cliffs, NJ: Prentice-Hall.

Szasz, T. (1964) *The Myth of Mental Illness*. New York: Harper & Row.

11 Power and Politics

Power can be defined in a number of ways. C. Wright Mills (1956) stated that: 'It is the ability of an individual or a group to bring about visible change in the behaviour of other people.' This power can be seen in institutions and Chapter 5 has demonstrated the exercise of power as described by A. Etzioni (1964), that is by use of coercion, remuneration, or moral pressure. Another way of classifying power is that used by Urry and Wakeford (1973) which has three aspects: economic power based on the control of economic resources, political power based on the control of resources of force, and cultural power based on the control of society's norms and values.

Power, therefore, cannot exist in isolation, it has to be seen in a specific context. Worsley (1964) has argued that as it does not exist in itself, it can only be seen in its effects and that everybody has some of it, some area of choice, even if this power is in itself negative, that is the power to veto or to 'vote with one's feet'. However, some people have overwhelming and decisive power and this is frequently institutionalized.

POLITICS

The study of politics is usually considered to be the study of power. However, this definition produces problems as power can be seen at work in all areas of society, schools, factories and tennis clubs as well as within the state. Max Weber defined the state as 'a human community which successfully claims the monopoly of the legitimate use of force within a given territory.' This definition is useful in the discussion as it limits it to a defined geographical area — the state — and describes power which is supported by force, for example the police or the army, in a manner to which the inhabitants of the area have agreed. The fact that this power is 'legitimate' does not mean it is democratic or even popular with people, but in that they have either elected the government or, at the worst, not overthrown it, and in that they continue to live within its jurisdiction, it is 'legitimate'. This immediately raises the problem of the minority in any state. John Stuart Mill talked about the 'tyranny of the majority' and even in a democratic state this situation exists. In the United Kingdom no matter which party gains the most seats in an election, there will be a large number of the population, quite often a majority in terms of actual votes, who did not give the party their support. It is this situation which is the basis of the present debate on the need for electoral reform. Before looking at the system in more detail, it is necessary to return to the basic factors which, according to Bottomore (1964), are vital in the study of politics in a modern state.

The first of these is the need for the general population to be a 'political community'. In the present day, there is evidence that the ordinary citizen is becoming more aware of the problems associated with his community and this results in the second point, the need for political parties and *pressure groups*. Political parties are not new and neither are pressure groups, but today there appear to be more obvious signs of groups of people trying overtly to affect political decisions. These range from groups which lobby their Members of Parliament, through those who stage public demonstrations and marches, to the groups who feel that only violence will have any effect. The third requirement is that the government should be elected by universal adult suffrage. In democratic states, there are several political parties competing for power, while in a totalitarian state, choice is restricted to one candidate from among several, all of whom represent the ruling party. Both claim that they are consulting the people! Finally, Professor Bottomore sees the necessity for a centralized bureaucracy, in the case of Britain, the Civil Service, to administer public affairs and to maintain authority when governments change. Such an organization collects taxes, maintains legal standards, protects the public's health and many other activities that concern a modern industrialized country.

In Britain, therefore, we have the following political system which is concerned with the maintenance of the social system. Firstly, there is the Parliament which is the main policy-making body. Policy is then executed by the Civil Service and local government, backed by the police, the judiciary and the courts, which ensure that the policies are carried out. In some cases, local government may initiate policy which is at variance with that decided by the central government. The decision by a few councils to retain selective schools against the central policy of comprehensive schooling was an example.

Despite the claim by Britain to be a democratic state, it is frequently asserted that the country is governed by a body of élites and that the ordinary man can have little effect on the decisions made by government. There is in fact support for the Marxist idea of a 'ruling class' by considering the type of people who are elected Members of Parliament, their social class and type of education.

However, quite apart from political parties, there exist many groups which endeavour to exert pressure on the government to influence its decision-making. These may be economic groups such as associations of industry, for example the Confederation of British Industry, or the trade unions, which are associations of workers. The power of trade unions as a pressure group has been considerable, especially if representing a vital industry, and the effect of the 1973 miners' strike on the Conservative Government is an important example. However, their current power seems to be waning, most unions showing a fall in membership (Figure 15).

Moral or religious groups may also exert pressure. The

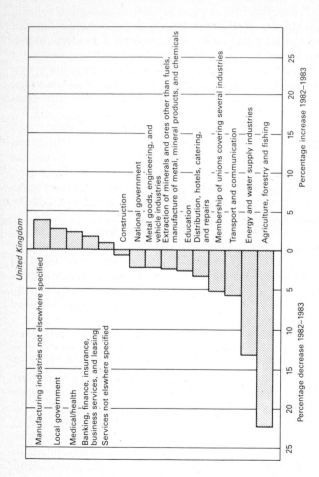

Figure 15. Change in trade union membership: by industry, 1982–1983. *Source:* Employment Gazette, Department of Employment.

Church of England has a direct voice in government via the House of Lords, but there are other groups, such as the Lord's Day Observance Society, which act as watchdogs on specific problems. Other groups may be formed to deal with a specific issue such as the Abortion Law Reform Society or the Campaign for Nuclear Disarmament, and, when their aim has been achieved, may be disbanded. Frequently, the Government will consult suitable groups before legislation is considered, so that the views of all parties may be seen to be sought.

One of the important aspects of political power is the relationship between the support they achieve and social class. However, the allegiance is not clear cut. There are many working-class Conservatives and a somewhat smaller number of social classes 1, 2 and 3 vote Labour. Even within the parties there tends to be division on specific issues. For example, some Conservatives are in favour of comprehensive education, which is a Labour policy, while within the Labour Party there are numbers who personally oppose nationalization of industry as a policy. The divisions are even less clear since the advent of a third group, the Liberal and Social Democratic Party Alliance. These variations are not usually clearly reflected in the voting of Parliament because of the mechanism of 'the Whip'. This ensures that members support their own party on vital policies, despite their personal views. It is tempting to think of Gilbert and Sullivan's Admiral who:

> . . . always voted at my party's call
> And never thought for myself at all
> I though so little, they rewarded me
> By making me an Admiral of the Queen's navy.

The question can be a thorny one when a free vote is allowed. An outstanding example of this was the Common Market Referendum, when members of both parties banded together on opposing sides. The idea of a referendum may appear to be the most democratic of all methods in deciding issues, but it is not often used in the United Kingdom. One of the major objections is that the voter may neither have sufficient knowledge nor, in certain cases, be able to see the implications sufficiently to make an informed decision. Another argument against it is that it is the Government's job to govern!

Public opinion is in fact frequently vague about major issues and research has shown that the effect of the mass media, including television, is not as great as might be hoped! Nevertheless, there are occasions when the government is aware that there are certain things that the public will not stand. This climate of opinion becomes particularly important as an election draws near, and is the basis for many of the parties' election manifestos.

Another problem is whether it can ever be said that the party in power is really representing a majority of the country's electorate. The present 'first past the post' constituency system may, and indeed frequently does, result in a government which may have the greatest number of elected Members of Parliament, but if the total votes for itself against the total votes of the opposition parties are considered, it may have a minority, not a majority of the total votes cast. It is because of this anomaly that the Alliance are seeking to introduce electoral reform and a system of proportional representation.

The link between the social and political systems is debatable. Some argue that, via the economic system, all societies which industrialize tend to protestantism and democracy, while others see a mass society eventually leading to a totalitarian state but, as we have shown in other chapters, this is not inevitable and a plurality of systems is the most likely outcome.

DISTRIBUTION OF POWER

Sociologists usually use one of three ways to explain how power is exerted in society, that is, ruling class, élitism or pluralism.

Ruling Class

In Chapter 6, we discussed Karl Marx's model of the development of social class, based on the access to the means of production producing economic dominance. Those with this access to economic dominance inevitably wielded the power and thus became the ruling class. Central to this thesis is the concept of solidarity within the classes, so that members of the economically powerful class act together to dominate those without access to this economic power, even though they too are a group with a self-conscious solidarity.

Élitism

This also assumes that power is in the hands of relatively few people but in this case, those without power are not seen as possessing solidarity, but are a disorganized mass.

Élites can be formed in a variety of ways, but are almost always characterized by a privileged level of education, professional expertise and other forms of merit. Many conceive of this group as being well disposed to society at large, making decisions and exercising power for the greater good of society, while others visualize them as working for their own ends.

Although not a cohesive class, as in Marx's model, it is generally assumed that the various groups of élites nevertheless do have many shared values and are most commonly members of the upper middle or upper classes.

Pluralism

This view rejects the notion of the concentration of power in the hands of small specific groups, or a ruling class, and sees society made up of a large number of groups which conflict and/or cooperate, so that power does not remain static but ebbs and flows from group to group in time and for specific purposes. To achieve this situation, there is an underlying assumption that there is a consensus in society as to what is 'good' for society, and that therefore any power exerted will be appropriate and useful to enable society to achieve its goals (note the reification of society that occurs in this argument). This pattern of power is assumed to occur where there are free electors, political equality for the electorate, free speech, and the concept of a welfare state.

POWER AND HEALTH CARE

In a welfare state, where the health care system is nationalized, it may be said that those working within it have little power as they are employees of the system as well as potential consumers. In addition, the majority may be loosely described as 'professionals' and, as is shown in Chapter 6, one of the characteristics of professionals is service to others, rather than power for themselves. However, this view is hotly contested by many who see the professionalization of any occupational group as a mechanism to develop an élitist state and hence exercise power. George Bernard Shaw epitomized this view when he wrote 'All professions are conspiracies against the laity.'

Certainly, anyone reading the history of the National Health Service cannot but be struck by the way the medical profession has been able to act as a pressure group in order to protect itself and achieve its own ends. This is demonstrated from the compromises that Bevan had to make to get medical participation in setting up the NHS, through to the present day.

Attempts to modify this power by the setting up of the Community Health Councils and Patient Participation Groups have met with only small success, and even these groups tend to comprise middle-class activists, so that many groups, such as the mentally handicapped, chronically sick and elderly, still have little power over the way their health is catered for. This debate is of particular interest when considering the allocation of resources for preventative services and health promotion versus provision for acute illness intervention.

The difficulty is that doctors have access to knowledge that is not easily possessed by the ordinary man and, as such, have power. Vicente Narvaro (1976) argues that medicine supports capitalism because it obscures the true cause of ill health, social deprivation and environmental misuse. Therefore, their legitimate claim to power, the improvement of health, is challenged and the claim made that most advances in health in the last one hundred years have been as a result of public health measures rather than medical intervention.

Similar arguments have begun to develop regarding the professionalization of nursing. Some groups, such as the Radical Nurses and Radical Midwives, claim that nurses display similar arrogance over their patients, imposing their standards of care on those unable to assert themselves and ask for different consideration. This danger is obvious and must be guarded against; perhaps the use of the nursing process, plus a model of nursing theory which requires patient participation in identifying need, planning and executing care, and finally evaluating what has been achieved, will prevent this inappropriate exercise of power developing (see page 64).

It is often claimed that the nurse is, or should be, the patient's advocate. If this is so, then the need for understanding and acceptance of the patient's point of view becomes obvious. Nurses, unlike doctors, tend not to be very politically aware and yet, as the largest group employed within the health service, they are in a position to function as a large pressure group over vital issues. One of their complaints is that they feel it is not possible to strike because of the danger to the patient and so they are powerless. This is not so, as the Royal College of Nursing's 'Raise The Roof' Campaign (1969/70) showed. On this occasion, mass lobbying of MPs and public marches in London and all other major cities and towns produced a public awareness of the low pay of senior staff and resulted in an inquiry and, eventually, an award being made. Unfortunately, as public sector employees, nurses are particularly prone to government restrictions on pay. The fact that the National Health Service is a monopoly employer further limits their power in pay bargaining. Other governmental decisions, such as the reduction in hours worked by junior hospital doctors, and rates of pay and the decision to phase out pay beds, have resulted in groups of doctors taking industrial action, either 'work to rule' or strikes. This is a new development, cutting across the idea of the professional putting the needs of the client first and also the concept of service being its own reward, so that money is less important.

Nurses have not yet been involved in industrial action to any great extent, indeed it is against the policy of the Royal College of Nursing, and this does, to some extent, limit their power.

The imposition of general managers in the health service following the Griffiths Report has further reduced the power of nurses at organizational level and demonstrated how a government can ignore the requests of nurses that they retain a voice at policy level. It is too early to comment on the RCN's campaign in this respect. Part of the problem appears to have been the inability of nurses to realize early enough the implications of the recommendations.

Nursing power appears, therefore, to be small, compared with that of doctors, partly because, as a very large and disparate group, nurses rarely speak with one voice, but have various factions, regional or related to area of practice. Indeed, the passing of the 1979 Nurses' Act nearly foundered on its passage through Parliament because of pressure groups made up of some of these factions.

Until nurses reach the level of political sophistication in which they appreciate that there is strength in numbers, it is likely that they will remain weak and unable to influence government or other professional groupings, to the extent that, taking into account their numbers, they should.

References and Further Reading

Alford, R. (1975) *Health Care Politics*. Chicago: University of Chicago Press.

Benn, S.J. & Peters, R.S. (1971) *Social Principles and the Democratic State*. London: Allen and Unwin.

Bottomore, T.B. (1964) *Elites and Society*. Harmondsworth: Penguin.

Etzioni, A. (1964) *Modern Organisations*. Englewood Cliffs, NJ: Prentice-Hall.

Illich, I. (1976) *The Limits to Medicine*. London: Marion Bayars.

Maxwell, R. & Weaver, N. (eds.) (1984) *Public Participation in Health*. London: King's Fund Publishing.

Mills, C. Wright (1956) *The Power Elite*. Oxford: Oxford University Press.

Navaro, V. (1976) *Medicine Under Capitalism*. London: Croom Helm.

Rose, R. (1965) *Politics in England*. London: Faber & Faber.

Salvage, J. (1985) *The Politics of Nursing*. London: Wiley.

Shaw, G.B. (1906) *The Doctors' Dilemma*. London.

Urry, J. & Wakeford, J. (eds.) (1973) *Power in Britain*. London: Heinemann.

White, R. (1985) *Political Issues in Nursing*, Vol. I. London: J. Wiley.

White, R. (1985) *The Effects of the NHS on the Nursing Profession, 1948–1961*, London: King's Fund Publishing.

Worsley, P. (1964) *Sociological Review*. Monograph No. 8.

12   Social Change

Social change has been a focus of interest and debate since Comte postulated the law of three stages. He suggested that all societies passed through the stages of theological thought (largely concerned with superstitions) via a metaphysical phase to a positive stage, that is, an era of scientific thought. This evolutionary approach to social change was akin to the evolutionary theories being postulated at the time by Darwin in the biological sciences. Marx argued that ideological social change resulted from change in the infrastructure of society, that is change in the means of production, while Weber felt ideological change came first, as in his theory of the rise of capitalism following the development of the Protestant ethic.

In recent years the main interest has centred on the transition of societies from a pre-industrial to an industrialized state and to a situation which may be described as post-industrial. Along with this change in the techniques of production, society tends to become modernized; that is, it develops a high level of education, health care and civil administration. Although modernization usually follows industrialization in that a high level of production and hence gross national product is required to finance the changes, some societies have been able to achieve aspects of modernization such as education and health care as a result of external aid and prior to their industrialization. The fact that material and non-material factors do not always keep in step has been described by Ogburn (1922) as *cultural lag*: for example, non-material benefits such as reduced death rates tend to fall behind material benefits such as high wages. The point of real interest is what actually triggers off the change and what are the prerequisites. For example, industrialization always results in changes in education but in some societies the educational changes appear to occur first; which, therefore can be said to be the pre-condition, and which the consequence, or may either occur?

Sociologists who follow a *functionalist* perspective would assert that society changes in response to its needs and therefore the educational system changes as society needs more highly educated people. Such a view will tend to see all societies taking the same steps and eventually reaching a degree of homogeneity. Thus *convergence theory* states that as societies become industrialized they will tend to become alike in terms of social stratification and social institutions. Such a theory takes little account of the fact that societies may commence industrialization from different points and that societies developing at the moment are unlikely to take the same steps as those societies that developed early. Equally, all types of political control, stratification patterns and belief systems can be found in industrial societies.

The functionalist approach therefore implies that change in any one area of society will lead to adjustive changes in other areas so that integration is maintained. Durkheim, for example, saw society as a way of thinking, feeling and acting which was external to the individual (society is *sui generis*) and exerting pressure on the individual to conform. This pressure to conform was felt due to a *collective consciousness*, that is, shared norms and values resulting from socialization. As we saw in Chapter 1, when this consensus breaks down then the ensuing conflict or normlessness leads to anomie.

Such theories tend to over-emphasize consensus in society, whereas sociologists argue that conflict is not only common in society but may itself act as an integrating force. The effect of war on society tends to produce a sinking of internal differences while the external enemy is fought. Lack of consensus without conflict is a fairly common experience, for example the motivation to nurse may come from a desire to care for individuals, a desire to accumulate knowledge, or as a means of social mobility, yet the individuals with these different goals may each be an excellent nurse and work together as a team. Social change is also stimulated by the expectations of individuals and groups, and their interaction. Although Dahrendorf asserts that 'social change is the result of the shifting balance of power between interest groups', ideologies and value systems are vital in affecting the way an individual sees any aspect of change and therefore how he responds to it. In some circumstances conflict will be absorbed and although individuals may feel discontent this will not become organized and will not affect society.

One aspect of conflict is that described by Marx which he said was derived by the ownership or non-ownership of the means of production. He felt that the increasing poverty of the workers would eventually lead to polarization of society into two classes, the proletariat and the bourgeoisie, who would come into open conflict. The warring of the classes would eventually lead to overthrow of the bourgeoisie and the production of a 'classless' society. Dahrendorf, while agreeing in many ways with Marx, feels that the crux of the question is the possession of power and therefore the class struggle is over the ability to regulate conditions of work and to dispose of the material profits.

Conflict may occur between religious groups and if this also coincides with class or political differences, then the accumulation of conflicting ideologies may make it more intense; an excellent example of this exists in Northern Ireland today. Overt demonstrations of conflict as in a strike may act as a safety-valve providing an outlet for accumulated frustrations. Conflict may therefore be institutionalized, that is, regulated by agreed rules as in the 'collective bargaining' relationship between the trade unions and the employers. Individual conflict with society's norms and values is often displayed by behaviour which is described as deviant. This term, which frequently carries derogatory overtones, may be applied to reformers and revolutionaries, hippies or homosexuals as well as to drug addicts and thieves. In fact the use of the term will vary with the society as it is applied to those who violate society's norms and what is acceptable in one society may be taboo in another. Society expects its members to pursue socially valued goals by socially approved means. Where social pressure to conform is very strong there is likely to be resistance to any form of innovation and change will be inhibited. Deviance in society is probably normal and a demonstration of the fact that power is not repressive. The position of the deviant in some countries clearly demonstrates that there power is repressive, for example, consider the way the intellectual deviant is contained in Russia by defining him as mentally ill. The social aspect of deviance is important as there is the danger of regarding occurrences like drug addiction, alcoholism and suicide as purely medical or psychological problems. This frequently results in a treated individual being returned to the pressures in society which caused the first deviation, and unless these are dealt with the likelihood of a relapse is high. In all types of deviance, including crime, there is probably a complex interaction between social, psychological and, in some instances, biological factors and therefore all must be taken into account in any programme of punishment, treatment or rehabilitation. Not all social frustration or pressure leads to deviance of a pathological nature. History is full of the achievements of the socially deprived who have seen their deprivation as a spur rather than a handicap. In other cases the deviance of an individual has resulted in invention, innovation and social change.

NATIONALISM

It often comes as a surprise to the visitor to the United Kingdom that it is made up of four quite distinctive countries with their own culture and even remnants of their own language. The development of nationalistic movements in these countries has increased in momentum in recent years. Some of the impetus has come from the allocation of scarce resources, for example Scottish oil or Welsh water, and some from the feeling that cultural differences were being overridden. Social solidarity is maintained by emphasizing the 'differences' that exist. While in the United Kingdom children are not taught to 'salute the flag' as occurs in the United States, there is a respect for the monarchy and government taught both overtly and via the study of history. There is also a degree of nationalism, encouraged, again overtly and covertly, by the use of patriotic songs such as *Rule Britannia* and this is continued into public life by the use of the National Anthem at football matches, theatres and other public occasions. In Wales, for example, not only is there a strong move to preserve the language but in schools Welsh history gets pride of place and on public occasions the Welsh Anthem is sung before *God Save the Queen*. At an extreme level, the British laws are considered to be 'illegitimate' as they do not represent Welsh interests.

The 1979 Nurses, Midwives and Health Visitors Act recognized these national boundaries by providing four statutory boards, one for each country (England, Northern Ireland, Scotland and Wales), as well as a UK Central Council. As the main function of these boards is nursing education, national needs and differences can now be taken into account.

A MULTIRACIAL SOCIETY

Another of the major changes to occur in Great Britain since the war has been the influx of the members of many nations. In most of the discussions so far no account has been taken of the fact that the individual might be black or white, a native of the country or an immigrant. Yet in most Western societies, including Britain, the ethnic origin of the individual does affect the way he is regarded by society and it is therefore yet another way that society can be changed.

The differential treatment of persons ascribed to certain categories is called *discrimination* and is demonstrated to a greater or lesser extent by a great proportion (according to one survey two-thirds) of the British population to the large number of immigrant races to be found. At the lowest level this discrimination is antipathy, in which case action for or against the immigrant is avoided. At its most extreme it is prejudice, an emotional, irrational, rigid disposition, usually resulting in hostile behaviour.

Reasons for this discrimination are difficult to define. It may be linked with Britain's colonial past where the coloured person was the servant and therefore of the lowest social class. Another view is that coloured people are seen as archetypical strangers, both in appearance and behaviour, in a society in which mild xenophobia (fear of strangers) is the norm. This produces problems for the British-born coloured person who may be two or three generations removed from the original immigrants.

Obviously the reason the immigrant entered the United Kingdom will affect perception of the host country. Reasons vary from overpopulation and unemployment to persecution, either religious or ideological (for example West Indians feel that Britain is home and expect a welcome!). On entering the United Kingdom, immigrants have to contend with a new language (even if English is the native tongue as in the West Indies). Then a new culture which affects marriage norms (in many cases the position of women in Britain cuts across previous cultural or religious requirements), food, weather, clothing and housing. Often it is impossible for them to get a mortgage and high rents may be imposed even by landlords of their own race. Frequently they are condemned to run-down areas of cities (called 'twilight zones') and thus form ghettos. Overcrowding by British standards is common, and smells of cooking are often offensive to the neighbours. When seeking work such immigrants are usually unskilled by United Kingdom standards or their qualifications are not acceptable and hence there are problems with trade union prohibitions. There is a great deal of evidence that coloured people are discriminated against when applying for jobs and when seeking promotion.

Later there is the problem of education of children. Discipline at school is often not considered adequate and 'play' a waste of time. As they may not want to lose their own culture, in some instances health may suffer due to inadequate diet, women may be afraid of outside contacts and folk remedies are often used because the administration of the National Health Service is not understood. Social isolation is often experienced as the host population may not wish to mix with immigrants socially even if they tolerate them at work. This lack of personal friendship is often commented on by immigrants who join local churches, as is the lack of emotion displayed by the British in their religious services. The lack of family or neighbourly support frequently results in hardship amongst individual immigrants, especially as they may not understand the social services and feel that they have no-one to whom they can go for help.

All studies show that racial discrimination is most obviously demonstrated towards coloured immigrants — those with negroid features suffering most. The reason for this is uncertain. Possibly they are the most obviously 'different' group and certainly this discrimination is perpetuated even to second and third generation British subjects who have this appearance.

With all immigrants a degree of adaptation takes place as they accept the culture of the host society. The speed with which this takes place and the effectiveness of the resocialization vary with age and whether the immigrant intends to return to his country of origin. For example, many Pakistanis come to Britain for a few years, so that they can send money home to their family, but since they intend to return home they do not mix with British society and only adapt to it sufficiently to earn their living.

If the immigrant has to learn to adapt, then the host society must learn to accept and this often requires a modification of its organizational framework. Problems arise when a country's legal system contains items which conflict with the immigrants' beliefs. An example of this is the legislation relating to the wearing of crash helmets and the requirements of Sikhs that they wear a turban. At another level, the move to make schools co-educational has resulted in Pakistani

Muslim families refusing to allow their teenage girls to be educated with boys.

The ultimate state of adaptation by the immigrant and acceptance by the host is usually seen when physical amalgamation takes place via marriage. When this occurs assimilation can be said to be complete. However, many ethnic groups do not wish this stage to be reached as they fear the disappearance of their own culture and, as far as coloured–white mixed marriages are concerned, there is still prejudice and discrimination both to the partners and their children.

It might be thought that health care is an area where racial discrimination is less likely to be practised, as the codes of ethics of medical and nursing staff emphasize the worth of the individual regardless of colour, class or creed. However, difficulties still arise due to prejudice and lack of knowledge of the reasons for beliefs and actions. They can occur either way in that a white patient may object to a coloured nurse, or a white nurse dislike caring for coloured patients.

Even where different ethnic groups exist apparently happily side by side, there is often discord beneath the surface waiting to erupt. Two sociologists researching in Birmingham, Rex and Moore (1967), assert that: 'Prejudice is linked with competition for scarce resources such as houses or "jobs" and in a period of recession it is more likely to show itself openly and explode into violence.'

Western civilization has failed to solve the problems created by multiracial societies and a great deal more needs to be done to modify deep-seated attitudes of fear and distrust of those who are 'different'.

CULTURE AND HEALTH CARE

It is vital for a nurse to be able to appreciate the 'perception' of her patients, particularly when they are of a different background to herself. The previous chapters have indicated the variation in perception that may result from class differences, different patterns of socialization and education. This section, however, will concentrate on differences related to ethnic origin. Such differences are increasing in importance as the British community contains many distinctive ethnic groups.

One of the fascinations of nursing is that although throughout the year the diagnostic record of patients in a ward or as part of a case load in the community may appear repetitive, each patient has presented with a different set of problems. All nurses have experienced the patient who lies quietly in bed uncomplaining despite the presence of a painful condition, while in the next bed another patient, with apparently less wrong with him, groans and cries and demands constant attention. While there may be biological and psychological reasons for these variations, quite often they are due to socialization patterns related to ethnic origin. The use of words is often related to normative base, for example cold soup is related to the individual's concept of hot soup and not to an absolute temperature reading. Feeling ill or well is not an absolute condition but the perception or description of the condition is coloured by the individual's emotional state and that is most clearly illustrated in the area of pain. Cultural patterns frequently determine whether pain is accompanied by the stiff upper lip of the British or by the outward crying of the Latin races. Measurement of pain level, even within the groups mentioned, is difficult; between them, almost impossible.

The totality of human experience and its effect on perception and performance in any specific situation has been referred to on many occasions. It might be thought unnecessary to discuss the effect of culture on nurse–patient interaction as in any given country the nurse and patient will probably share a common culture, hence a common set of definitions. The mobility of nations is such that if this were once true it is no longer, and most countries now contain within their population many distinct races, each with their own philosophy, code of conduct, traditions and myths. Even within one race there are differences and in Great Britain the Celts and Anglo-Saxons, the Yorkshire man and the man of Kent, the East Anglian and the Cornishman all adhere to that mysterious 'something' which makes them appear different when outside their own area. Within large towns there are differences between the East and West 'enders', relating not merely to social class but to philosophy of life, use of words, patterns of child care and so on.

Before actually getting to specific health care there may arise difficulty over names. The British tendency to ask for Christian and surname produces problems in non-Christian groupings. For example, all Sikh men appear to be Mr Singh and all Sikh women Miss or Mrs Kaur. This is due to the fact that at baptism a boy is known as Singh and a girl, Kaur, to indicate that they are a member of the brother- or sisterhood of Sikhs. Equally confusing is the fact that first names are chosen by random opening of the holy book of Ad Granth. This means male and female children may have the same names. Medical record-keeping in these cases is hazardous.

There is great danger that the nurse will attach a moral value to the beliefs and practices of individuals whose background is different from her own. However, her ways of doing things may seem just as strange, irrational and superstitious to members of another culture as theirs do to her. An example of this lack of understanding between cultures occurred when nutritionists in America, who felt that meals ought to be properly balanced in every twenty-four hour period, assumed that Italian children in their community were getting inadequate food. To compensate they introduced more milk into the children's diets and were distressed when the children became too fat, because their meals balanced over a week and not twenty-four hours. Refusal of food offered may be due to religious dietary laws, for example, no orthodox Jew or Moslem is permitted to eat pork and no Hindu is permitted to eat beef, or it may be due to unfamiliarity or just dislike of taste. Where possible, attempts should be made by the nurse to ensure a well-balanced diet using foods that are both acceptable and familiar (strange tastes are obviously not well tolerated by a person who is ill) and often the patient's family will be only too happy to prepare and bring in a tempting dish when the hospital facilities fail.

The Pakistani, whether from Pakistan or Bangladesh, is usually a Moslem and frequently comes from a rural area. It is common for sons of farming families to take it in turn to spend a few years in Britain, during which time they send money home to help the extended family from which they originated. Family ties and obligations are very strong and they are used to a community of the type described by Tönnies as *Gemeinschaft*. Men and women have distinct roles and these are maintained despite the pressures of the host country. Alexander (1974) points out that although the position of women in a Moslem society may cause anger by supporters of women's liberation, these women are unquestionably queen in their own homes and feel very secure in their role in that they know what is expected of them and are able to meet these expectations satisfactorily. Pressure to conform to the role of a Western woman, in particular the need to go out and mix with men, a practice not common in Pakistan, may produce severe conflict and even mental breakdown (as stated, this also produces problems in the education of girls). A Moslem woman may therefore refuse to be examined by a male doctor and would be unlikely to tolerate the presence of a male nurse.

Moslems are required to fast during the month of Ramadan, which means abstinence from food and drink between sunrise and sunset; the strict observer may even spit out his own saliva. Although sick or nursing mothers are not obliged to keep this fast some may wish to do so. Problems may also arise with regard to diabetics or those involved in occupations where they perspire heavily. However, with sympathetic advice it is possible to help these people observe their religious duty, hence contributing to their spiritual happiness. The pig is an unclean animal to the Moslem and they will not eat any of it, a point to be considered in hospital diets. Other meat has to be killed in a special way by a 'halal' butcher who may be found in areas where a large number of Moslems reside. Otherwise relatives may help to provide food.

Pakistani welfare associations exist in many areas, as charity is a tenet of the Moslem faith, and these may be mobilized to help the family in distress. The role of the health visitor is vital to the women whom she has to try to prevent becoming prisoners in their own homes, thus not availing themselves of help and advice on infant-feeding, childrearing or educational problems.

Indians may come from any area of that continent but, like the Pakistani, tend to come from extended families living in villages where they know everyone. Like the Pakistani, they have a prudish approach to sex, deviance is not tolerated and the woman's place is in the home. Those who come from the Gujarat are generally Hindus. These people have a high standard of hygiene (often higher than their British hosts), regard the cow as a sacred animal and therefore will not eat beef, and some do not eat any type of meat. Because of this many of their diets may be short in protein and they need to be encouraged to eat cheese and eggs and to drink milk.

The Sikhs who come from the Punjab also will not eat beef but do eat other meats. They also refrain from smoking. Much publicity has been given to the fact that the adult male is required to wear a turban and this has caused difficulty with respect to legislation relating to crash helmets. Such a difficulty may also develop in hospital if nurses try to enforce rules, especially prior to surgical procedures. This conflict is rarely necessary and merely requires a flexible approach.

One major area of conflict in both Pakistani and Sikh families results from the education of their children in British schools. Naturally the patterns of socialization they experience at home and school are different and this may produce tension and even mental illness in the participants. Attempts to avoid this conflict may help account for hostile or withdrawn attitudes in some immigrants. Although they have faced the change resulting from leaving their own country it may be that this can only be tolerated if the family remains secure in its traditional structure in the host country.

West Indians present quite a different picture. Friendly and outgoing, they usually arrive with the idea that they will be easily accepted into the community and are greatly disillusioned when they find this is not so. To the nurse they may appear irresponsible as, although obviously loving their children, they frequently leave them alone or with a child-minder (often unregistered) while mother goes to work or out to enjoy herself. Attitudes to health tend to be equally casual, antenatal visits are often deferred until late in pregnancy — after all, childbirth is a 'natural' event so why should it take place in a hospital which is for ill people? Encouragement by the health visitor will be needed to ensure that children are immunized and protected from the dangers in the home.

The fact that a proportion of West Indians live together without a legal marriage may be traced back to the past when slaves were not allowed to marry and indeed couples were often separated by their owner selling one of them. Hence, in a family several children may each have a different father which may be a problem if there is any question of inherited disease. As with the slaves, so now many West Indians have a deep religious belief which finds expression in joyful, colourful, modes of worship. The Pentecostal movement, with its emphasis on spontaneity and singing, particularly appeals to them.

All these groups lack the support of friends and family that they might have received in their own lands and therefore they frequently show signs of stress. Not only do they suffer from anomie due to the variation in norms and values but they are also faced with the problems of housing, work, food and language. It is therefore not surprising that there is a high level of mental illness amongst immigrants. Research in Nottingham in 1973 (Alexander, 1974) showed that over a seven-year period 29% of all new cases of schizophrenia came from immigrant groups although they only comprised 6.5% of the total population.

The loneliness of the single immigrant and the stress they experience may result in them seeking an outlet for their tension in promiscuous relationships. Venereal disease therefore tends to be high amongst single immigrants, who may also be reluctant to seek advice.

Understanding as to the reason for illness is often based on folklore, as indeed it is amongst many of the host population, and many have little or no immunity to diseases they may encounter in the city life in which they live. Tuberculosis is therefore common amongst immigrants from rural areas who are often living in slum conditions and have a poor diet.

All these comments are related to immigrants in the United Kingdom but Western habits have often spread to other areas of the world with disastrous results. Recently it has been found that mothers in some areas of Africa have ceased to breast-feed their babies, preferring to use the Western 'baby-milk'. These are expensive so are usually made up with more water than instructed and so babies which would have been well-nourished on breast milk are now suffering from deficiency diseases due to inadequate protein. This is an example of the adoption of one aspect of modernization without the others, such as education and health supervision, that would have prevented this disaster.

Again, while in our culture barrenness is a misfortune it is not the disaster that it is in some cultures where the woman will be divorced, disgraced and virtually an outcast if she does not produce children and, in particular, sons.

Hospitals in the West tend to regard peace and quiet as a necessary requisite for recovery even though this means separation from family and friends. In other cultures the sick person is supported by the presence of the family and is never left alone, and to die without members of the family present would be unheard of. Nurses who have cared for Romany families in the United Kingdom will know that the whole clan usually wishes to be involved in the care and treatment of a loved one, a fact that may cause difficulties in an open ward but can be coped with if a single room is available.

While nurses are not expected to know all about every

culture in the world it is important that an open mind is kept about beliefs and customs and that rules are not so strictly enforced that distress is caused over matters that may be unimportant. Instead of branding a patient as uncooperative or unreasonable, a little time should be spent discovering the reason for the attitude, the deeply held traditions, the fears, or the taboos, then difficulties can often be solved and all patients will feel equally respected and cared for.

Only when the nurse is fully aware of her own cultural position will she be able and willing to accord respect to individuals who eat, speak, and fear differently from herself.

SECULARIZATION

'Man, my Lord (Bishop Wilberforce) is a being born to believe' said Benjamin Disraeli.

Few would wish to disagree with this statement for where groups of people are studied a central core of values can be found round which they cohere and which governs their activities. Indeed, each person reading this chapter holds personal beliefs about life, death, right, wrong, good and evil and these have been formed as a result of socialization, education and experience. Beliefs are therefore both part of culture and formed by it and therefore tend to have an interdependence, thus constituting a system rather than an unrelated set of isolated values.

Obviously there are various types of belief systems in society, such as those related to religion, science, politics and morality. Some of these, such as scientific beliefs, or beliefs in the effect of certain actions, are able to be tested. For example, it is possible to believe that the Earth is round and to demonstrate this fact by not falling off but returning home when sailing from east to west. Equally, a belief that marriages between individuals of different races are wrong might be thought to be substantiated by divorce rates or discrimination against children. Other beliefs may be less easily proved, such as those about the nature of God, or standards of morality.

When beliefs and ideas are related to actions they frequently undergo simplification (and occasionally falsification) to reflect the needs of a specific group. This clustering of beliefs is called an 'ideology' and acts as a legitimation for action. An ideological statement is often one where a value judgement is disguised as a statement of fact. Most organizations, whether secular or religious, are governed by an ideology which motivates their members to action and acts as the central focus.

Although cultures vary, many of them have beliefs which are similar. On the other hand, individuals within one society may have quite different beliefs. The study of the reasons for these similarities and differences is called the sociology of knowledge. Marx argued that man's beliefs were determined by material conditions and experiences as a result of the relationship to the means of production. This unity of ideas formed 'class consciousness'. Although this is a deterministic view of beliefs, Marx admitted that sometimes the proletariat could hold the ideologies of the bourgeoisie, a fact that Engels called 'false class consciousness'. Today there are still differences in ideology between social classes (as was shown in Table 9), which indicates variations in working- and middle-class perspectives.

Beliefs therefore may be related to specific needs of individuals or groups in that they may serve to explain the situation in which they find themselves. For example, a belief in a better life after death may help a person endure hardship and deprivation in this life (hence the reason Marx described religion as the 'opium of the masses'). Patients in hospital often express beliefs in an effort to explain their illness, either positively or negatively. Frequently a patient will say: 'I've always lived a good life and don't deserve this illness' or, 'What have I done to deserve this?', both statements indicating a belief that illness is related to wrong-doing as a form of punishment. Alternatively, 'only the good die young' may help make sense of a painful situation. In some cultures 'magic' may be the explanation of crop failure, or natural disasters such as floods. Religion can assist man to make sense of his environment and explain and relieve tension created by uncertainty. This is very important in the care of the sick when distress can be caused if explanation as to the nature of the illness is not understood. A patient's approach to mental illness can sometimes be affected by reference to the New Testament accounts of 'devil possession'.

The care of the terminally ill and the approach to the dying patient and his relatives will of necessity be affected both by beliefs of the staff and patient, and the role of the hospital chaplain may be vital at this crisis point. In a cosmopolitan society the nurse should try to develop an awareness of the basic beliefs of other ethnic groups as these may affect death rites and ceremonies and these should be respected.

Religion has played a part in political decisions over the years, particularly when there is a direct link as in Britain where bishops sit in the House of Lords. Pressure may be exerted when laws related to such matters as birth control, abortion or euthanasia are considered but even over these matters there is often dissent within the Church and therefore its voice is muted. However, in some Roman Catholic countries such as Italy or Spain the pressure exerted by church leaders on politicians may be considerable.

Scientific belief is a body of knowledge which can be tested and verified. It is not restricted to any specific culture or community but shared by the worldwide community of scientists. However, it can be affected by beliefs in other areas, witness the political ideologies which try to muzzle scientific progress in some countries. Equally it may come into conflict with religious beliefs and the Church.

As already discussed, Weber demonstrated the differences in ideology following the Reformation and the way this affected economic behaviour, arguing that the Protestants' belief in hard work and thrift was a major force in the development of capitalism.

The relationship between religious and social ideology in Britain today is hard to assess as outward religious observance declines yet belief in God is still held by many (Tables 15 and 16). Martin (1969) says that 'the gospel remains relevant but the Church may be superannuated'. Despite the general decline in Church attendance, many people preserve the traditions of Church weddings, baptisms and funerals — possibly a superstitious belief in the *rites de passage*.

There is quite a lot of evidence to show that industrialization assists in this process of *secularization*, which is the process whereby religious thinking, practice and institutions lose social significance. Instead of the church or chapel providing the focus of entertainment and political activity, other agencies develop to meet these needs. This change is particularly obvious in the Welsh chapels which used to provide the centre for music in the area and allowed many a budding politician to develop his strength as an orator while acting as a lay preacher.

Although religion may act as a focal point for society and therefore be a unifying factor it can be divisive, in that it divides believers from non-believers, Protestant from Catholic. Various branches of the Christian Church are divided on specific issues such as birth control, political issues and war. However, within ethnic subcultures religion is often a source of identification, for example Jewish communities are linked by their adherence to the Torah.

The relationship between religious beliefs and morality is important. If rules are derived from theology, then they are in some respects 'sacred', so to break them is heresy; thus change is resisted. The problem arises when religion is declining. For a time morality may be retained without questioning but eventually will need a fresh form of legitimation. This is the situation in many Western countries today and the result has been marked changes in acceptable behaviour. Debate on the care of handicapped babies, such as use of life-support machines, transplant surgery and 'the right to die', reflect changing views on the value of life.

Table 15. Membership (in thousands) of churches and other religions in the United Kingdom.

	1975	1980	1985*
Christian churches			
Anglican	2272	2166	2058
Presbyterian	1717	1574	1483
Methodist	596	536	485
Baptist	267	237	226
Other Trinitarian churches†	584	609	758
Total Protestant†	5436	5122	5011
Roman Catholic	2436	2344	2265
Total Christian	7872	7466	7276
Percentage of adult population‡	18.4	16.9	16.0
Non-Trinitarian churches			
Mormons§	80	91	102
Jehovah's Witnesses	80	84	92
Spiritualists	57	52	53
Other Non-Trinitarian	88	90	101
Total	305	317	348
Other religions			
Muslims	400	600	900
Sikhs	115	150	175
Hindus	100	120	140
Jews	111	111	111
Others	85	147	198
Total	811	1128	1524

* Projected.
† Includes Orthodox churches.
‡ Population aged 15 or over. The 1985 percentage has been calculated using 1981-based population projections.
§ Church of Jesus Christ of Latter-Day Saints.
Source: UK Christian Handbook 1985/86, MARC Europe.

Table 16. Baptisms and confirmations (in thousands) in selected churches.

	1961	1971	1981	1984
Church of England				
Infant baptisms	412‡	347[»][«]	219	202§
Other baptisms	11‡	8[»]	39	37§
Confirmations	191	110	90	80
Church of Scotland				
Infant baptisms	45	32	22	19
Other baptisms	5	2	2	2
Admissions by profession of faith*	33	18	14	12
Church in Wales				
Baptisms			16	15
Confirmations	12	8	8	7
Baptist churches†				
Baptisms of believers	6	5	7	7
Methodist churches				
Baptisms	46	36	29	29§
Confirmations	24	12	11	9§
Roman Catholic churches				
Baptisms under age 7	131	103	74	72
Other baptisms	14	6	3	2
Confirmations	88	83	58	47

* This approximates to confirmation.
† Churches affiliated to the Baptist Union of Great Britain and Ireland.
‡ 1960.
» 1970.
« Since 1978 'infant baptisms' have been specified as baptisms of children under one year of age to relate more realistically to figures for live births. Previously the designation 'infant baptism' was left to the discretion of the priest baptizing the child.
§ 1983.
Source: The Churches.

In Conclusion

Throughout this book evidence has been presented which implicitly and explicitly shows that society is in a constant state of change: changes in levels of employment/unemployment, the role of women, political parties, power, organizational structures, the structure of the family, life expectancy (Table 17) and so on. Indeed, it would be odd if this were not so as change in one section of society inevitably produces a reaction and change in another as a new level of stability is sought. At no time can society be considered as a static entity, instead it is a dynamic, ever-changing collection of people, groups, institutions and organizations.

As with society, so with that section of it called 'nursing'. The activity of providing care is itself affected by social expectations, pressures and provisions. This is the fascination of the study of sociology, which seeks to explain, anticipate and record these changes.

References and Further Reading

Alexander, B. (1974) Help for immigrant families. *Nursing Times*, **70**, 17.

Argyle, M. (1975) *The Social Psychology of Religion*. London: Routledge & Kegan Paul.

Bottomore, T.B. (1964) *Elites and Society*. Harmondsworth: Penguin.

Butterworth, E.D. (1969) Two cultures. In Butterworth, E.D. & Weir, D. (1970) *The Sociology of Modern Britain*. London: Fontana.

Helman, C. (1984) *Culture, Health and Illness*. Bristol: John Wright.

Martin, D. (1969) *A Sociology of English Religion*. London: Heinemann.

Merton, R.K. (1957) *Social Theory and Social Structure*. New York: Free Press.

Ogburn, W.F. (1922) *Social Change*. New York: Viking Press.

Patterson, S. (1962) *Dark Strangers*. Harmondsworth: Penguin.

Rex, J. & Moore, W. (1967) *Race, Community and Conflict*. Oxford: Oxford University Press.

Rose, R. (ed.) (1966) *Studies in British Politics*. London: Macmillan.

Table 17. Expectation of life in the United Kingdom, from birth and from specific ages.

		Males						Females					
		1901	1931	1951	1961	1971	1981	1901	1931	1951	1961	1971	1981
Expectation of life*													
From birth		48.0	58.4	66.2	67.9	68.8	69.8	51.6	62.4	71.2	73.8	75.0	76.2
From age	1 year	55.0	62.1	67.5	68.6	69.2	69.6	57.4	65.1	72.1	74.2	75.2	76.1
	10 years	51.4	55.6	59.1	60.0	60.5	60.8	53.9	58.6	63.6	65.6	66.5	67.2
	15 years	46.9	51.1	54.3	55.1	55.6	55.9	49.5	54.0	58.7	60.6	61.6	62.3
	20 years	42.7	46.7	49.5	50.4	50.9	51.2	45.2	49.6	53.9	55.7	56.7	57.4
	30 years	34.6	38.1	40.2	40.9	41.3	41.6	36.9	41.0	44.4	46.0	47.0	47.6
	40 years	26.8	29.5	30.9	31.5	31.9	32.0	29.1	32.4	35.1	36.5	37.3	38.0
	45 years	23.2	25.5	26.4	26.9	27.3	27.5	25.3	28.2	30.6	31.9	32.7	33.3
	50 years	19.7	21.6	22.2	22.6	23.0	23.1	21.6	24.1	26.2	27.4	28.3	29.0
	60 years	13.4	14.4	14.8	15.0	15.3	15.6	14.9	16.4	17.9	19.0	19.8	20.6
	65 years	10.8	11.3	11.7	11.9	12.1	12.4	11.9	13.0	14.2	15.1	16.0	16.7
	70 years	8.4	8.6	9.0	9.3	9.5	9.5	9.2	10.0	10.9	11.7	12.5	13.2
	75 years	6.4	6.4	6.7	7.0	7.3	7.4	7.1	7.4	8.0	8.7	9.4	10.0
	80 years	4.9	4.8	4.8	5.2	5.5	5.5	5.4	5.4	5.8	6.3	6.9	7.3

* Further number of years which a person could expect to live.
Source: Government Actuary's Department.

Saunders, L. (1954) *Cultural Differences and Medical Care*. New York: Russell Sage Foundation.

Susser, M. & Watson, W. (1971) *Sociology in Medicine*. Oxford: Oxford University Press.

Wilson, B.R. (1961) *Sects and Society*. London: Heinemann.

Worsley, P. (Ed.) (1972) *Problems of Modern Society*, Part 9. Harmondsworth: Penguin.

Appendix

EDWARDS PERSONAL PREFERENCE SCHEDULE

A brief description of the need dimensions measured by the EPPS follows:

1. Achievement: to do one's best, to be successful, to accomplish tasks requiring skill and effort, to be a recognized authority, to accomplish something of significance.
2. Deference: to get suggestions from others, to find out what others think, to follow instructions and do what is expected, to praise others, to tell others they have done a good job.
3. Order: to have written work neatly and well organized, to make plans before starting on a difficult task, to have things organized, to keep things neat.
4. Exhibition: to say witty and clever things, to tell amusing jokes and stories, to talk about personal adventures and experiences, to have others notice and comment upon one's appearance.
5. Autonomy: to be able to come and go as desired, to say what one thinks about things, to be independent of others in making decisions, to feel free to do what one wants.
6. Affiliation: to be loyal to friends, to participate in friendly groups, to do things for friends, to form new friendships, to make as many friends as possible.
7. Intraception: to analyse one's motives and feelings, to observe others, to understand how others feel about problems, to put oneself in another's place.
8. 'Succourance': to have others provide help when in trouble, to seek encouragement from others, to have others

be kindly, to have others be sympathetic and understanding about personal problems.

9. Dominance: to argue for one's point of view, to be a
leader in groups to which one belongs, to be regarded
by others as a leader.

10. Abasement: to feel guilty when one does something
wrong, to accept blame when things do not go right, to
feel that personal pain and misery suffered does more
good than harm, to feel the need for punishment for
wrong-doing, to feel better when giving in and avoiding
a fight than when having one's own way.

11. Nurturance: to help friends when they are in trouble,
to assist others less fortunate, to treat others with kind-
ness and sympathy, to forgive others.

12. Change: to do new and different things, to travel to
meet new people, to experience novelty and change in
daily routine, to experiment and try new things, to eat
in new and different places, to try new and different jobs.

13. Endurance: to keep at a job until it is finished, to complete any job undertaken, to work hard at a task, to
keep at a puzzle or problem until solved.

14. Heterosexuality: to go out with members of the opposite
sex, to engage in social activities with the opposite sex,
to be in love with someone of the opposite sex, to kiss
those of the opposite sex.

15. Aggression: to attack contrary points of view, to tell
others what one thinks about them, to criticize others
publicly, to make fun of others.

Glossary

Achieved status. A social position obtained by the individual's own effort.

Affectivity. Related to emotions and feelings.

Alienation. This describes the feelings of an individual who perceives himself as unable to control or affect his own destiny. It was originally used by Marx to describe the lack of control that the industrial worker has over his labour and product. Powerlessness.

Altruistic. Behaviour which is for the good of others.

Anomie. The condition of the individual who is no longer secure in his pattern of life and does not understand the norms of the society in which he is situated. Used by Durkheim to explain one situation in which an individual may commit suicide. Normlessness.

Ascribed status. A social position accorded because of an individual's birth rather than his effort.

Authority. The legitimate power accorded to an individual or group on traditional, charismatic or rational grounds.

Bias. Weighting to one side. May be due to an individual's own values or preconceived ideas.

Bourgeoisie. Used by Marx to indicate the class of people who had control over the means of production.

Bureaucracy. A hierarchical form of organization first described by Weber.

Charisma. A personal attribute of an individual which is recognized by others, who will follow his leadership.

Class. Used to describe a way in which society may be divided. Frequently linked to occupational categories.

Class consciousness. Awareness by an individual of his class position. Originally used to describe the united feelings of the workers in relation to those who controlled them.

Collective consciousness. The feelings shared by a specific social group.

Community. A shared way of life located in a defined geographical area.

Concept. An abstract idea.

Consensus. Agreement.

Continuum. A sequence of events. A continuous scale of characteristics used in measurement.

Convenience sample. Items or people selected for testing because of their ease of access.

Convergence theory. This states that as societies industrialize their social institutions will become alike.

Correlation. The relationship of two items. May be positive, that is, the two items will occur together and change together; or negative, as when item one increases the other item decreases.

Cultural lag. The time taken for cultural change to spread throughout a given area or society.

Culture. The norms, values, life-styles of a specific society.

Definition of the situation. The interpretation or meaning given by an individual to the social situation in which he is placed.

Delinquency. Criminal activity of a minor character.

Demography. The scientific study of human populations, such as size, birth rates, housing, etc.

Deviancy. Behaviour outside the norms or limits set by a specific society.

Discrimination. Distinguishing different groups of people or factors. Frequently used to indicate a different form of behaviour towards a specific group of people.

Dynamism. Moving, changing. Used to indicate a non-static situation in society.

Egoistic. Concerned with oneself. Selfish.

Elite. The best. A superior group.

Embourgeoisement. Relates to the theory that all social classes are becoming alike.

Empirical. Information gained through the senses, or by experience.

Expressive. Outward demonstration, usually related to feelings.

Extended family. A married couple, their children and one or more direct relatives. Usually related to three generations or more living together.

Function. A necessary or integral part of something.

Functionalism. A social theory which sees specific social factors or occurrences as 'necessary' to that society's existence.

Gemeinschaft. Used by Tönnies to describe a closely integrated community.

Generalized other. The grouped ideas (values, norms, etc.) attributed by an individual to those with whom he interacts.

Gesellschaft. Used by Tönnies to describe a loosely integrated form of association.

Group. Two or more persons linked by a common characteristic, goal or belief.
Primary group — face-to-face relationship — small.
Secondary group — large, held together by weak ties of common purpose or belief.

Homeostasis. A term used to describe changes which occur in man to maintain balance. Used in sociology to indicate a self-regulating mechanism in society.

Hypothesis. A supposition made on the basis of reasoning. A statement to be tested.

Ideal-type. An abstract set of characteristics. Not found in any particular example but contains all the factors that may logically be present. Used as a point of comparison.

Ideology. A set of concepts and beliefs which are held to explain social phenomena, not necessarily true.

Infrastructure. The economic base of society which affects the development of institutions.

Institutions (social). Specific forms of organization and interaction occurring in society, e.g. education.

Instrumental. Useful. Activity that achieves a specific task.

Internalization. Learning norms, roles and symbols in such a way that they become part of normal behaviour. This learning often occurs at a subconscious level.

Labelling. The process by which individuals may be categorized according to social behaviour or any other attribute, diagnosis is an example of a specific type of labelling.

Latent function. The hidden or secondary effect of a specific act.

Legal/rational. Authority legitimated by rules to which the individual has consciously or unconsciously given assent.

Life-style. A pattern of behaviour related to economic commodities.

Macroscopic view. Broad overall view.

Manifest function. The overt reason for a specific act.

Microscopic view. Detailed view of a small area.

Mobility (social). Movement up, down, or across the social stratification system.

Model. A conceptual framework capable of explaining or illustrating a complex situation. May be verbal, diagrammatic or mathematical.

Morbidity. The incidence of illness or disability in a population.

Multiple roles. Refer to the various positions occupied by any individual at one time.

Neonatal. Relating to the first four weeks of life.

Norms. Recognized standard.

Nuclear family. Consists of a husband, wife and their children in one residence.

Particularism. Viewing each situation as unique.

Peer group. An association of members of one's own age.

Power. The ability of an individual or group to bring about change in the behaviour of other people.

Pressure group. An association of people with a common interest who endeavour to persuade others (often government) to action which will further the group's goals.

Prestige. The level of standing and influence of a specific group.

Primary socialization. The initial learning process which occurs within a family.

Profession. A term applied to occupations which are able to demonstrate specific characteristics including specialized knowledge and skill, and autonomy of action.

Proletariat. The common people; the lowest class in the community. Used by Marx to describe the working class.

Protestant ethic. An ideology developed by Calvin at the time of the reformation which stressed the value in the sight of God of hard work and the accumulation of money. Weber saw it as the factor which stimulated the emergence of capitalism.

Random sample. Each item has equal chance of being selected.

Reification. The act of endowing inanimate objects with life.

Relative deprivation. Deprivation of material or spiritual factors measured against groups of a similar type.

'Rites de passage'. Ceremonies that accompany a change in an individual's status, e.g. marriage.

Role. The part an individual plays as a result of occupying some position in life.

Role discrepancy. The situation that arises when more is expected of an individual than his ability allows.

Role-set. The various facets of response required by a specific role.

Sanctions. Adverse actions applied to an individual who does not adhere to society's norms.

Secondary socialization. Learning that takes place after early childhood.

Secularization. The process by which religious influences decrease in their effect.

Self-fulfilling prophecies. Behaviour from an individual or group which develops as a result of the expectation of its development by others — originally absent.

Significance. Used to show that research findings have meanings and are not just the result of a chance occurrence.

Significant other. A person whose attitudes and values have a marked effect on the attitudes and values of another individual.

Social class. *See* Class and Stratification.

Social exchange. The demands and rewards made and offered by individuals as they interact.

Social fact. Way of thinking or acting which commonly occurs in the specific society.

Social integration. The level at which an individual patterns his actions and beliefs on those of the specific society.

Social structure. The pattern of society and the institutions occurring within it.

Social system. The interaction of the individuals within a specific society according to a set of shared definitions.

Socialization. The process by which a culture is learned.

Status. Social position.

Status passage. Moving from one social position to another during the course of a career.

Stereotype. A set image of an object, individual, or group.

Stigma. Imputation of an adverse type attached to an individual indicating that the person is not 'normal'.

Stratification. The hierarchical position occupied by an individual or group in society relative to others.

Stratified sample. Selection to ensure all groups are represented.

Subculture. A subdivision of a national or larger culture.

Suprastructure. Aspects of society such as education or law which depend on the economic infrastructure for their development.

Task allocation. A nurse is usually given one or more tasks to carry out for all the patients requiring such attention, e.g. all the pressure area care, all the mouth toilets.

Team nursing. A small number of nurses carrying out all the care for a small group of patients.

Theory. A statement describing the relationships between phenomena or concepts which have been shown (by research) to exist. May be used to explain empirical findings.

Therapeutic community. Relates to an environment which allows an individual to 'act out' unacceptable behaviour and then develop more suitable responses. Usually used in connection with psychiatric illness.

Total institution. A setting in which an individual carries out all of his daily activities, e.g. the army, a prison, or custodial care mental hospital.

Total patient care. Implies one or two nurses carrying out all the care required by the patient.

Traditional leadership. Handed down in a predetermined manner, e.g. father to son.

Universalism. Oriented towards all aspects of society, not a specific part.

Index

AIDS (acquired immune deficiency syndrome), 142
Alexander, B., 188, 190
Alienation, 59
Alter, 36
Altschul, A.T., 113, 151
Ambulation, early, 123
Anderson, E.R., 113
Anomie, 9, 179
Anticipatory definition of situation, 57
Anxiety, 66–7
Association, 27
Authority
    administrative, 58 (fig.)
    charismatic, 56
    legal, 56
    organization and, 56–7
    professional, 58 (fig.)
    rational, 56
    traditional, 56
    see also Power

Baber, M., 152
Bed position in ward, 67
Bereavement, 161
Bias, 15
Biological sciences, 2
Boore, J., 67, 160
Bottomore, T.B., 168–9
Bourgeoisie, 180
Brown, G., 110–11

Bureaucracy, 49–50
Burns, T., 55

Child abuse, 32
Cinema, 139–40
Class consciousness, 80, 193
    false, 193
Classification of Occupations, Registrar General's, 78, 79 (table)
Class variations in family life, 80–1
Coercive power, 147
Collective consciousness, 179
Committee on Nursing (Briggs Report, 1972), 113–14
Committee on Senior Nursing Staff Structures (Salmon Report, 1966), 118
Commune, 28, 28–9
Communication, 65–70
    non-verbal, 66, 147–9
    verbal, 147–9
Community, 27–32
    hospital, 29
    latent function, 28
    manifest function, 28
    therapeutic, 29
Community Health Council, 174
Comparative method, 14–15
Competent medical health, 40–1
Compliance, organization and, 56–7

Comte, A., 1, 178
Concept, 4–5
Conflict in society, 179–80
Congruent power/compliance
    patterns, 64 (table)
Consciousness of self, 34
Cultural lag, 178
Culture, 82
    health care and, 185–92
    subculture group, 40

Dahrendorf, 179–80
Darwin, C., 72–3
Davies, K., 100
Death, 162–4
    nurse's perception, 163
    person living alone, 30
Death rate, neonatal, 18
Demographic material, 13
Dependency, stigmatizing/
    humiliating, 131
Deviance, 20, 45–6
    in society, 181
Discrimination, 182
Disraeli, B., 192
Divorce, 19, 103 (fig.)
Divorce Reform Act (1969), 103
Doctors
    inability to understand work-
      ing class patients, 66
    National Health Service
      domination, 97
Documents, historical/other,
    12–13
Durkheim, E., 5, 7–9, 27–8, 179
Dying, 162–4, 194
Dynamism, 6

Economics, 3
Education, 83–5
    comprehensive, 84
    cycle of deprivation, 85–6

government policy, 88–9
    immigrants' attitudes, 189
    middle-class values, 85
    Plowden Report (1967), 88
    Robbins Report (1963), 86
    social class and, 81–6
    United States, 83, 85
Education Act 1870, 83
Education Act 1944, 83
Edwards Personal Reference
    Schedule (Appendix I),
    145, 202–3
Ego, 36
    development, 37
Élitism, 173
Elkin, F., 35
Embarrassment, 149–52
Embourgeoisement, 99–100
Empathy, 152–5
Employment agency, 122
Engels, F., 193
Etzioni, A., 56, 167
Expectation of life in UK, 199
    (table)

Family, 16–32, 37
    attitude to sickness/hand-
      icap, 30–1
    extended, 17, 19–20
    geographic proximity, 24–5
    ideal-type, 24
    middle-class, 25
    nuclear, 17, 20–1, 24
    single-parent, 22, 23 (table)
    status passage, 18
    working class, 24–5
Food, religious attitudes to,
    187–9

Gender, 102–12
Gemeinschaft (community), 27,
    188

General Electric Company, Hawthorne Works, 54
General manager, 52, 121
General practitioner, persons consulting (England & Wales), 96 (table)
Geography, 3
Gesellschaft (association), 27
Gift
    ability to return, 127
    patient to nurse, 127
Glaser, B.G., 162
Goals, 55, 58
    displacement, 122
    Maslow's specifications, 124–5
Goffman, E., 36, 60, 63, 149
Group
    primary, 62
    small, 62–5
    subculture, 40

Hall–Jones scale, 78
Handicapped child, family reaction to, 30–1
Hayward, J., 67, 160
Hinton, J.M., 163
History, 3
Holistic medicine, 97
Homeostasis, 14
Hospital
    as community, 29
    as organization, 49–71
    goals, 119
    self-maintenance, 120
Hospital chaplain, 194
Houseman (junior hospital doctor), 122

Ideal-type, 17
Ideology, 193

Illness
    chronic, attitudes to, 44–5
    concepts, 41
    long-standing, males reporting (1972), 96 (table)
    persons reporting (England & Wales, 1976), 95 (table)
    stages, 41
Immigrants
    illness in, 191
    schizophrenia in, 190
Infant mortality (England & Wales, 1975/6), 94 (table)
Institutions, 22–4
    environmental effect, 69–70
    long-stay, working the system, 65
    total, 63–4
Interaction situation, 155 (fig.)
Internalization, 37
Interview, 12

Japan, industries and family relationship, 25
Job-enrichment, 74

Kibbutz, 29
King, I.M., 155, 156

Labelling, 141–2
Labour pains, cultural attitudes to, 126
Language use, working-class/middle-class homes, 80–1
Leaders
    expressive, 63
    instrumental, 63
Life-style, 77–80
Lorber, J., 111

Magic Mountain, The, (T. Mann), 64

Marriage, 17–18
  childhood, 19
Martin, D., 195
Marx, K., 73, 77–8, 179, 180, 193
Maslow, A.H., 124
Mass communications, 134
Maternal deprivation, 32
McCall, G.J., 154
McFarlane, J.K., 113
Mead, G.H., 34, 36
Medical care, stages, 41
Mental illness, 45
  family attitude, 31
Menzies, I.E.P., 150
Methods of investigation, 9–13
  historical/other documents, 12–13
  interview, 12
  observation, 10–11
  questionnaires, 11–12
  sampling, 9–10
Methods of study, 7–15
Middle-class mother, 80–1
Milestones, 159
Mill, J.S., 168
Mobility, 20
Model, 13–14
Moore, W., 185
Moore, W.E., 100
Moslems, 188–9
Mothering, 31–2
Multiplicity of contacts 131–2
Multiracial Society, 182–5

Narvano, V., 175
National Boards for Nursing, Midwifery and Health Visiting, 76
National Health Service, domination by doctors, 97
Nationalism, 181–2

Non-cooperation, 64
Non-family group, 25–6
Norms (rules) of society, 8
Nurse
  academic, 108
  American student, 146
  closer relationship with patient, 151–2
  depersonalizing of service, 150
  English student, 145–6
  factors affecting role, 119
  'flight from the bedside', 118
  involvement with patient, 154
  male, 107, 108–9
  medically orientated, 116
  motivation, 115–17
  perception, 144–6
  perception of death, 163
  personality traits of student nurses, 144–6
  political power, 175–6
  primary, 119
  professional organizations, 76
  rewards, 120
  ritual task performance, 150
  social anxiety, 150
  stressful situations and their relief, 118
  Swedish, 116
  talking to patient, 123
  task allocation, 113
  television presentation of, 138
  uniform, patients' reactions, 68–9
  unique function, 113
  what nurses do, 117–24
Nurse–doctor relationship, 105–8, 120–1
Nurse–patient interaction, 124–6

as social change, 126–32
psychiatric field, 151
Nurses, Midwives and Health
  Visitors Act 1979, 176,
  182
Nursing
  as occupation, 113–33
  as university subject, 82
  displacement of goals, 122
  function, manifest/latent,
    123
  models, 114
  private, 128–9
  'task-centred' activity, 118
  theories, 114
Nursing area with districts, 51
  (fig.)
Nursing management
  'pyramid', 50 (fig.), 57

Observation, 10–11
Ogburn, W.F., 178
Open University courses, class
  bias, 86 (table)
Organization, 49
  ideal-type, 49
Organizational structures
  mechanical, 55
  organic, 55

Pain, cultural attitudes to, 186
Pakistanis, in Britain, 184–5,
  188–90
Parliament, British, 169, 171
Parson, T., 36, 40
Patient
  attitudes to hospital admis-
    sion, 42, 46–7
  bad health enjoyed, 125
  cultural variations, 126
  dignity, 69

early ambulation, 123
essential to nurse's job satisfaction, 131
expectation of nurse, 154
gift to nurse, 127
goal, 124–5
help given by, 131
length of stay in hospital, 123
physical contact with other
  person, 68
popular/unpopular, 142–3
preoperative preparation,
  misunderstanding of
  instructions, 67–8
reaction to dependency, 125
role adoption, 40
role in hospital, 42–5
socialization into hospital,
  58–62
steps in becoming, 43 (fig.)
stigma of dependency, 128
total care, 113
treated as child, 69
world of, 16–33
Patient Participation Group, 174
Peer groups, 34
People
  generalized others, 36
  significant others, 36, 37
Perception
  factors determining, 156,
    157 (fig.)
  individual, 134
  shared, 155–6
Perspectives, working-class/
  middle-class, 90–1 (table)
Pinker, R., 128, 131
Plowden Report (1967), 88
Pluralism, 173–4
Political community, 168
Political science, 4
Politics, 167–72

Power, 167
  coercive, 56
  distribution, 172–3
  health care, 174–6
  normative, 56
  remunerative, 56
  see also Authority
Presentation of the self, 36
Press, the, 134–6
Pressure-groups, 169–71
Prestige, 39
Professionalism, definition of, 120
Professionals in health care, 74–6
Proletariat, 180
Protestant ethic, 72
Psychology, 2
Public opinion, 171–2

Questionnaires, 11–12

Radio, 137–9
Rahe, R.H., 159
Record keeping, 119
Referendum, 171–2
Reification, 14
Reiter, F., 148–9
Religion
  baptisms and confirmations, 197 (table)
  membership of churches and other religions, 196 (table)
  observance, 195
  part in political decisions, 194
Retirement, 22
Retreat, The (York), 29
Rex, J., 185
Robbins Report (1963), 86

Robinson, D., 41–2
Rogers, C.R., 153
Role, 35–47
  deviance, 39
  discrepancy, 39
  multiple, 38–9
  part of social system, 35
  personal property, 36
  playing, effect of interaction, 36
  typification, 36–7
Role-set, 38, 39 (fig.)
Role-taking, 153–4
Royal College of Nursing, 'Raise the Roof' campaign, 175
Ruling class, 173

Sample, 9–10
  convenience, 10
  quasi random, 10
  stratified, 10
Sanctions, 64
Schizophrenia, 31, 190
School, 37
School children, health of (Scotland, 1973), 94 (table)
School health services, use by children (Great Britain, 1965), 95 (table)
Scott, W.R., 154
Secularization, 192–5
Self appreciation, 61
Semi-professionals, 76
Sex Discrimination Act (1975), 103, 104
Shaw, G.B., 174
Shop floor, behaviour of workers, 54–5
Sikhs, 187, 189–90
Simmons, J.L., 154
Singh, A., 145

Situation, definition of, 5
Smart, 110
Snow, C.P., 82
Snow, J., 165
Social anthropology, 2–3
Social change, 178–99
Social class
    attitudes, 89–91
    health, 92–7
    status and power, 91–2
Social exchange, 126, 129, 130
        (fig.)
Social facts, 5
    illness related, 164–5
Social inequalities as essential
        for society, 100
Social integrations, 8
Socialization, 19, 34–5
    desire to belong, 37–8
    primary, 34
    secondary, 21, 34–5
    workers/inmates, 57
Social mobility, 97–9
Social philosophy, 3
Sociology, 1, 113
    convergence theory, 179
    functionalist view, 179
Sociotechnical system, 73
Sorokin, Piterim, 4
Stalker, G.M., 55
Statutory qualifications, 83
Stereotypes, 140–1
Stereotyping, 37
Stigma, 142–4
Stockwell, F., 142–3
Strauss, A.L., 162
Stress, 159–60
Stress-related diseases, 165
Suicide, 7–9
    altruistic, 8–9
    egotistic group, 9
Sweden, nurses in, 116

Team nursing, 113
Technical language, 66
Technology, 82
Television, 137–9
Tension reduction, 37
Terminology, 4–6
Theory, 4–5
Thomas, W.I., 134
Timasheff, N.S., 133
Timetables (J. Roth), 11
Token person, 109–10
Tönnies, F., 27, 127
Toys, working-class/middle-
        class children, 81
Trade unions, 93 (table), 169,
        170 (fig.)
    collective bargaining, 180
Tschudin, 110
Tuke, William, 29

Unemployment effects, 74
Uniform, nurses', patients'
        attitude to, 68–9
United Kingdom Central Coun-
        cil for Nursing, Midwif-
        ery and Health Visiting,
        76, 121
Universities' role, 82
University graduates by social
        class of fathers, 84 (table)
Urry, J., 167
Use of findings, 13

Value-free research, 15

Wakeford, J., 167
Ward sister, 52–4, 57, 122
Webb, C., 111
Weber, M., 49, 56, 72, 91, 167
Western habits, spread of, 191
West Indians, in Britain, 183,
        190

Wife(ves), number of, 18
Women
  as deviants, 111
  economic activity rates
    (1983), 106 (fig.)
  health care of, 110–11
  position in Moslem society,
    188
  position in Western society,
    102–3
  professional, 103–4
Word association, 74
Work
  attitudes to, 72–4

job-enrichment, 74
organization in industry, 73
Workers
  alienation, 73
  behaviour, 54–5
  powerlessness, 73
Working-class mothers, 80–1
Working the system, 65

Xenophobia, 183

Youth subculture, 86–8

Znaniechi, F., 134